RESTful Java Patterns and Best Practices

Learn best practices to efficiently build scalable, reliable, and maintainable high performance RESTful services

Bhakti Mehta

PUBLISHING

BIRMINGHAM - MUMBAI

RESTful Java Patterns and Best Practices

First published: September 2014

Production reference: 1150914

Published by Packt Publishing Ltd.
Livery Place
35 Livery Street
Birmingham B3 2PB, UK.

ISBN 978-1-78328-796-3

www.packtpub.com

Credits

Author
Bhakti Mehta

Reviewers
Dustin R. Callaway
Masoud Kalali
Kausal Malladi
Antonio Rodrigues

Commissioning Editor
Pramila Balan

Acquisition Editor
Vinay Argekar

Content Development Editor
Adrian Raposo

Technical Editor
Edwin Moses

Copy Editors
Janbal Dharmaraj
Karuna Narayanan
Alfida Paiva

Project Coordinator
Kinjal Bari

Proofreaders
Paul Hindle
Jonathan Todd

Indexers
Mariammal Chettiyar
Monica Ajmera Mehta

Graphics
Ronak Dhruv
Abhinash Sahu

Production Coordinator
Manu Joseph

Cover Work
Manu Joseph

About the Author

Bhakti Mehta is the author of *Developing RESTful Services with JAX-RS 2.0, WebSockets, and JSON, Packt Publishing*, published in 2013. She has more than 13 years of experience in architecting, designing, and implementing software solutions on top of Java EE and other related technologies. She is passionate about open source software development and has been one of the founding members of GlassFish Open Source Application Server.

Bhakti has a Bachelor's degree in Computer Engineering and a Master's degree in Computer Science. Her areas of research include architecting solutions for resiliency, scalability, reliability, and performance with respect to server-side technologies, web services, and cloud applications.

Currently, Bhakti is a Senior Software Engineer at Blue Jeans Network. As part of her current role, she works on developing RESTful services that can be consumed by ISV partners and the developer community. She also works on the backend infrastructure and is responsible for performance, scalability, and reliability of the services.

Bhakti is a regular speaker at different conferences and has authored numerous articles, blogs, and tech tips at different portals such as `https://home.java.net/` and Dzone. In her spare time, she enjoys kickboxing, traveling, and reading.

Bhakti's tweets can be followed at `@bhakti_mehta`.

Acknowledgments

Writing a book is a gratifying as well as demanding experience and I thank my family for putting up with my late nights and weekends while I was working on this book. I would like to acknowledge my husband, Parikshat, and my in-laws for their support. Thank you Mansi for always being so positive and standing by me when times got tough! This is for my two little kids who are a constant source of inspiration for me, to believe in the power of dreams and work hard to achieve them.

I would like to extend my gratitude towards my parents, my brother Pranav and his family for their encouragement throughout the course of the book's development. I am blessed to be surrounded by a group of very supportive friends especially from my undergraduate school days and would like to thank them for their motivation. Words cannot express my gratitude to all my wonderful colleagues at Blue Jeans Network and I truly appreciate their enthusiastic support and good wishes.

Thanks to the staff at Packt Publishing, especially Vinay Argekar, Adrian Raposo, and Edwin Moses for contacting me, reviewing the content, and keeping track of the schedule. Last but not least, I take this opportunity to thank the reviewers, Masoud Kalali, Dustin R. Callaway, Kausal Malladi, and Antonio Rodrigues, for their invaluable feedback and attention to detail.

About the Reviewers

Dustin R. Callaway is a software consultant, author, instructor, and full-stack developer. He currently works as a staff software engineer for Intuit Inc., a leading provider of financial software. He holds a B.S. degree in Computer Science from Brigham Young University and is the author of the book *Inside Servlets, Addison-Wesley*. His experience and interests include building RESTful web services with Java and Node.js as well as web and mobile applications.

Masoud Kalali is a Consulting Member of Technical Staff at Oracle. He is the author of the books, *Developing RESTful Services with JAX-RS 2.0, WebSockets, and JSON* published in 2013 and *GlassFish Security* published in 2010, both by Packt Publishing. He is also the author of numerous articles and quick references from Java.Net to Dzone.

Since 2001, when he started working in different software development roles, he has been blessed enough to work on multiple loosely-coupled architecture for high throughput message-based systems with JMS at heart and the rest of the components forming the stops around the JMS as the main messaging bus.

Performance analysis and performance consulting on architecture, design, code, and deployment configuration is another challenge he has spent some time working on. RESTful services and use of RESTful endpoints for data integration is one of the other practices he worked on for data integration for industry leading software systems: IJC and TIBCO Spotfire, during his work at ChemAxon.

Masoud has worked on security integration as another area, specifically in integration OpenSSO with a solid SOA framework used for developing BPEL flow-oriented software. At his current position at ORACLE, he works as the lead engineer in the design and development of application server and PaaS infrastructure of the ORACLE cloud service on top of both OVM/OVAB and Nimbula virtualization providers.

Masoud's Twitter handle is @MasoudKalali if you want to know what he is up to.

Kausal Malladi is a result-driven software engineer, inclined towards constantly exploring the latest advances in technology, to solve existing problems in the field of Computer Science and develop innovative products. He has done his Master of Technology in IT, specialized in Computer Science, from the International Institute of Information Technology, Bangalore (IIIT-B). He has more than two years of software design and development experience and is currently working at Intel.

At Intel, Kausal is a part of the Android Graphics Software Development team. He also worked for a couple of years in Infosys Ltd., before pursuing his Master's degree. At Infosys, he was part of an internal team that does R&D of effective solutions for challenging problems in the infrastructure space.

Kausal is an avid researcher, having more than six publications in reputed international journals. He also applied for a couple of Indian patents in 2013. He delivered a talk on *ATM Terminal Services the RESTful Way* at the *JavaOne India 2013* conference.

Kausal likes to play around with hobby projects in the areas of cloud computing and machine learning, apart from web development and open source advocacy. He is also passionate about music. In his free time, he listens to, sings, and plays (violin) Carnatic music. He also volunteers for the Society for Promotion of Indian Classical Music And Culture Amongst Youth (SPIC MACAY), a voluntary youth movement, both on organizational and technical fronts.

Visit `http://www.kausalmalladi.com` for more details about him.

Antonio Rodrigues is a software engineer with extensive experience in server-side development and mobile applications. In the past 17 years, he has worked with a range of companies including IT consulting companies, telecommunication companies, government agencies, digital agencies, and start-ups. He believes that APIs, in special Restful services, are crucial parts of software engineering in the current world of mobility.

You can follow Antonio on Twitter at `@aaadonai`.

www.PacktPub.com

Support files, eBooks, discount offers, and more

You might want to visit www.PacktPub.com for support files and downloads related to your book.

Did you know that Packt offers eBook versions of every book published, with PDF and ePub files available? You can upgrade to the eBook version at www.PacktPub.com and as a print book customer, you are entitled to a discount on the eBook copy. Get in touch with us at service@packtpub.com for more details.

At www.PacktPub.com, you can also read a collection of free technical articles, sign up for a range of free newsletters and receive exclusive discounts and offers on Packt books and eBooks.

http://PacktLib.PacktPub.com

Do you need instant solutions to your IT questions? PacktLib is Packt's online digital book library. Here, you can access, read and search across Packt's entire library of books.

Why subscribe?

- Fully searchable across every book published by Packt
- Copy and paste, print and bookmark content
- On demand and accessible via web browser

Free access for Packt account holders

If you have an account with Packt at www.PacktPub.com, you can use this to access PacktLib today and view nine entirely free books. Simply use your login credentials for immediate access.

Table of Contents

Preface

The confluence of social networking, cloud computing, and the era of mobile applications creates a generation of emerging technologies that allow different networked devices to communicate with each other over the Internet. In the past, there were traditional and proprietary approaches for building solutions, encompassing different devices, and components communicating with each other over an unreliable network or through the Internet. Some of these approaches, such as RPC CORBA, and SOAP-based web services, which evolved as different implementations for service-oriented architecture (SOA), required a tighter coupling between components along with greater complexities in integration.

As the technology landscape evolves, today's applications are built on the notion of producing and consuming APIs instead of using web frameworks that invoke services and produce web pages. This API-based architecture enables agile development, easier adoption and prevalence, and scale and integration with applications, both within and outside the enterprise.

The widespread adoption of REST and JSON opens up the possibilities of applications incorporating and leveraging functionality from other applications as needed. Popularity of REST is mainly because it enables building lightweight, simple, and cost-effective modular interfaces, which can be consumed by a variety of clients.

The advent of mobile applications calls for a stricter delineated client-server model. Companies that build applications on iOS and Android platform can consume the REST-based API and extend and deepen their reach by combining data from multiple platforms because of the REST-based architecture that is API centric.

REST has the additional benefit of being stateless, easing scalability, visibility, and reliability as well as being platform and language agnostic. Many companies are adopting OAuth 2.0 for security and token management.

This book aims to provide avid readers with an overview of the REST architectural style, focuses on all the mentioned topics, and then dives deep into best practices and commonly used patterns for building RESTful services that are lightweight, scalable, reliable, and highly available.

What this book covers

Chapter 1, REST – Where It Begins, starts with the basic concepts of REST, how to design RESTful services, and best practices around designing REST resources. It covers the JAX-RS 2.0 API to build RESTful services in Java.

Chapter 2, Resource Design, discusses different request response patterns; it covers topics such as content negotiation, resource versioning, and response codes in REST.

Chapter 3, Security and Traceability, covers advanced details in security and traceability around the REST API. It includes topics such as access control, authentication using OAuth, exception handling, and auditing and validation patterns.

Chapter 4, Designing for Performance, covers the design principles needed for performance. It discusses the caching principles, asynchronous and long running jobs in REST, and how to use the partial updates using PATCH.

Chapter 5, Advanced Design Principles, covers advanced topics such as rate limiting, response pagination, and internationalization and localization principles with detailed samples. It covers extensibility, HATEOAS, and topics such as testing and documenting REST services.

Chapter 6, Emerging Standards and the Future of REST, covers real-time APIs using WebHooks, WebSockets, PuSH, and Server-sent event services, and compares and contrasts them in various areas. Additionally, this chapter covers case studies demonstrating how the emerging technologies such as WebSockets and WebHooks are being used in real-time applications. It also outlines the role of REST with micro services.

Appendix, covers different REST API from GitHub, Twitter, and Facebook, and how they tie into the principles discussed in *Chapters 2, Resource Design,* through *Chapter 5, Advanced Design Principles.*

What you need for this book

To be able to build and run samples provided with this book, you will need the following:

- Apache Maven 3.0 and higher: Maven is used to build the samples. You can download Apache Maven from `http://maven.apache.org/download.cgi`.

- GlassFish Server Open Source Edition v4.0: This is a free community supported Application Server providing implementation for Java EE 7 specifications. You can download the GlassFish Server from `http://dlc.sun.com.edgesuite.net/glassfish/4.0/promoted/`.

Who this book is for

This book is a perfect reading source for application developers to get familiar with REST. It dives deep into the details, best practices, and commonly used REST patterns as well as gives insights on how Facebook, Twitter, PayPal, GitHub, Stripe, and other companies are implementing solutions with RESTful services.

Conventions

In this book, you will find a number of styles of text that distinguish between different kinds of information. Here are some examples of these styles, and an explanation of their meaning.

Code words in text, database table names, folder names, filenames, file extensions, pathnames, dummy URLs, user input, and Twitter handles are shown as follows: "GET and HEAD are safe methods."

A block of code is set as follows:

```
@GET
@Path("orders")
public List<Coffee> getOrders() {
    return coffeeService.getOrders();    }
```

When we wish to draw your attention to a particular part of a code block, the relevant lines or items are set in bold:

```
@Path("v1/coffees")
public class CoffeesResource {
```

```
@GET
@Path("orders")
@Produces(MediaType.APPLICATION_JSON)
public List<Coffee> getCoffeeList( ){
   //Implementation goes here

   }
```

Any command-line input or output is written as follows:

```
#  curl -X GET http://api.test.com/baristashop/v1.1/coffees
```

New terms and **important words** are shown in bold.

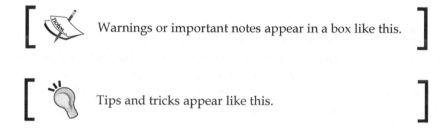

> [Warnings or important notes appear in a box like this.]

> [Tips and tricks appear like this.]

Reader feedback

Feedback from our readers is always welcome. Let us know what you think about this book—what you liked or may have disliked. Reader feedback is important for us to develop titles that you really get the most out of.

To send us general feedback, simply send an e-mail to feedback@packtpub.com, and mention the book title via the subject of your message.

If there is a topic that you have expertise in and you are interested in either writing or contributing to a book, see our author guide on www.packtpub.com/authors.

Customer support

Now that you are the proud owner of a Packt book, we have a number of things to help you to get the most from your purchase.

Downloading the example code

You can download the example code files for all Packt books you have purchased from your account at http://www.packtpub.com. If you purchased this book elsewhere, you can visit http://www.packtpub.com/support and register to have the files e-mailed directly to you.

Errata

Although we have taken every care to ensure the accuracy of our content, mistakes do happen. If you find a mistake in one of our books—maybe a mistake in the text or the code—we would be grateful if you would report this to us. By doing so, you can save other readers from frustration and help us improve subsequent versions of this book. If you find any errata, please report them by visiting http://www.packtpub.com/submit-errata, selecting your book, clicking on the **errata submission form** link, and entering the details of your errata. Once your errata are verified, your submission will be accepted and the errata will be uploaded on our website, or added to any list of existing errata, under the Errata section of that title. Any existing errata can be viewed by selecting your title from http://www.packtpub.com/support.

Piracy

Piracy of copyright material on the Internet is an ongoing problem across all media. At Packt, we take the protection of our copyright and licenses very seriously. If you come across any illegal copies of our works, in any form, on the Internet, please provide us with the location address or website name immediately so that we can pursue a remedy.

Please contact us at copyright@packtpub.com with a link to the suspected pirated material.

We appreciate your help in protecting our authors, and our ability to bring you valuable content.

Questions

You can contact us at questions@packtpub.com if you are having a problem with any aspect of the book, and we will do our best to address it.

1
REST – Where It Begins

Web services in the traditional SOA formats have been around for a long time to implement heterogeneous communication between applications. One way to support this kind of communication is to use the **Simple Object Access Protocol (SOAP)/Web Services Description Language (WSDL)** approach. SOAP/WSDL is an XML-based standard and works well when there is a strict contract between the services. We are now in the era of distributed services where different clients from the Web, mobile, as well as other services (internal or external), can make use of APIs exposed by different vendors and open source platforms. This requirement enforces the need for easier exchange of information between distributed services along with predictable, robust, well-defined interfaces.

HTTP 1.1 is defined in RFC 2616, and is ubiquitously used as the standard protocol for distributed, collaborative hypermedia information systems. **Representational State Transfer (REST)** is inspired by HTTP and can be used wherever HTTP is used. This chapter will go over the basics of the RESTful services design and show how to produce and consume RESTful services, based on the standard Java API.

This chapter covers the following topics.

- Introduction to REST
- Safety and idempotence
- Design principles for building RESTful services
- Java Standard API for RESTful services
- Best practices when designing RESTful services

Introduction to REST

REST is an architectural style that conforms to the web standards such as using HTTP verbs and URIs. It is bound by the following principles:

- All resources are identified by the URIs
- All resources can have multiple representations
- All resources can be accessed/modified/created/deleted by standard HTTP methods
- There is no state information on the server

REST and statelessness

REST is bound by the principle of **statelessness**. Each request from the client to the server must have all the details to understand the request. This helps to improve visibility, reliability, and scalability for requests.

Visibility is improved, as the system monitoring the requests does not have to look beyond one request to get details. **Reliability** is improved as there is no check-pointing/resuming in case of partial failures. **Scalability** is improved because the number of requests that can be processed by the server increases, as the server is not responsible for storing any state.

> Roy Fielding's dissertation on the REST architectural style provides details on the statelessness of REST. Check `http://www.ics.uci.edu/~fielding/pubs/dissertation/rest_arch_style.htm` for more information.

With this initial introduction to the basics of REST, we shall cover the different maturity levels and how REST falls in it in the following section.

The Richardson Maturity Model

The **Richardson Maturity Model** is a model developed by Leonard Richardson. It talks about the basics of REST in terms of resources, verbs, and hypermedia controls. The starting point for the maturity model is to use the HTTP layer as the transport. This is shown in the following diagram:

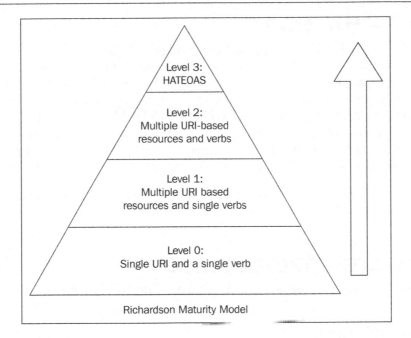

Level 0 – Remote Procedure Invocation

Level 0 contains SOAP or XML-RPC sending data as **Plain Old XML (POX)**. Only the POST methods are used. This is the most primitive way of building SOA applications with a single POST method and using XML to communicate between services.

Level 1 – REST resources

Level 1 uses the POST methods and instead of using a function and passing arguments it uses the REST URIs. So, it still uses only one HTTP method. It is better than Level 0 as it breaks a complex functionality into multiple resources with the use of one POST method to communicate between services.

Level 2 – more HTTP verbs

Level 2 uses other HTTP verbs such as GET, HEAD, DELETE, and PUT along with the POST methods. Level 2 is the real use case of REST, which advocates using different verbs based on the HTTP request methods and the system can have multiple resources.

Level 3 – HATEOAS

Hypermedia as the Engine of Application State (HATEOAS) is the most mature level of Richardson's model. The responses to the client requests contain hypermedia controls, which can help the client decide what is the next action they can take. Level 3 encourages easy discoverability and makes it easy for the responses to be self-explanatory. There is debate about whether HATEOAS is truly RESTful because the representation contains more information beyond just describing the resource. We will show details on how some platforms such as PayPal have implemented HATEOAS as part of their APIs in *Chapter 5, Advanced Design Principles*.

The next section covers safety and idempotence, the two important terminologies when dealing with RESTful services.

Safety and idempotence

The following section discusses in detail what are safe and idempotent methods.

Safe methods

Safe methods are methods that do not change the state on the server. For example, `GET /v1/coffees/orders/1234` is a safe method.

Safe methods can be cached. `GET` and `HEAD` are safe methods.

The `PUT` method is not safe as it will create or modify a resource on the server. The `POST` method is not safe for the same reasons. The `DELETE` method is not safe as it deletes a resource on the server.

Idempotent methods

An idempotent method is a method that will produce the same results irrespective of how many times it is called.

The `GET` method is idempotent, as multiple calls to the `GET` resource will always return the same response.

The `PUT` method is idempotent as calling the `PUT` method multiple times will update the same resource and not change the outcome.

`POST` is not idempotent and calling the `POST` method multiple times can have different results and will result in creating new resources. `DELETE` is idempotent because once the resource is deleted, it is gone and calling the method multiple times will not change the outcome.

Design principles for building RESTful services

Here is the process of designing, developing, and testing RESTful services. We will cover each of these in detail in this chapter:

- Identifying the resource URIs

    This process involves deciding what nouns will represent your resource.

- Identifying the methods supported by the resource

    This process involves using the various HTTP methods for CRUD operations.

- Identifying the different representations supported by the resource

    This step involves choosing whether the resource representation should be JSON, XML, HTML, or plain text.

- Implementing the RESTful services using JAX-RS APIs

    The API needs to be implemented based on the JAX-RS specification

- Deploying the RESTful services

    Deploy the service on an application container such as Tomcat, Glassfish, and WildFly. The samples show how to create a WAR file and deploy on Glassfish 4.0 and it can work with any JavaEE 7-compliant container.

- Testing the RESTful services

    Write the client API for testing the services or use curl-or-browser-based tools to test the REST requests.

Identifying the resource URIs

RESTful resources are identified by resource URIs. REST is extensible due to the use of URIs for identifying resources.

The following table shows sample URIs, which can represent different resources in the system:

URI	Description of the URI
`/v1/library/books`	This is used to represent a collection of book resources in a library
`/v1/library/books/isbn/12345678`	This is used to represent a single book identified by its ISBN "12345678"

URI	Description of the URI
`/v1/coffees`	This is used to represent all the coffees that are sold by a coffee shop
`/v1/coffees/orders`	This is used to represent all the coffees that are ordered
`/v1/coffees/orders/123`	This is used to represent a single order of coffee identified by "123"
`/v1/users/1235`	This is used to represent a user in a system identified by "1235"
`/v1/users/5034/books`	This is used to represent all the books for a user identified by "5034"

All the preceding samples show a clear readable pattern, which can be interpreted by the client. All these resources could have multiple representations. These examples of resources shown in the preceding table can be represented by JSON, XML, HTML, or plain text and can be manipulated by HTTP methods: GET, PUT, POST, and DELETE.

Identifying the methods supported by the resource

HTTP verbs comprise a major portion of the uniform interface constraint, which defines the association between the actions identified by the verb, to the noun-based REST resource.

The following table summarizes HTTP methods and descriptions for the actions taken on the resource with a simple example of a collection of books in a library.

HTTP method	Resource URI	Description
GET	`/library/books`	This gets a list of books
GET	`/library/books/isbn/12345678`	This gets a book identified by ISBN "12345678"
POST	`/library/books`	This creates a new book order
DELETE	`/library/books/isbn/12345678`	This deletes a book identified by ISBN "12345678"
PUT	`/library/books/isbn/12345678`	This updates a specific book identified by ISBN "12345678'

HTTP method	Resource URI	Description
PATCH	/library/books/isbn/12345678	This can be used to do a partial update for a book identified by ISBN "12345678"

The next section will cover the semantics of each HTTP verb in the context of REST.

HTTP verbs and REST

HTTP verbs inform the server what to do with the data sent as part of the URL.

GET

The GET method is the simplest verb of HTTP, which enables us to get access to a resource. Whenever the client clicks a URL in the browser, it sends a GET request to the address specified by the URL. GET is safe and idempotent. The GET requests are cached. Query parameters can be used in GET requests.

For example, a simple GET request to retrieve all active users is as follows:

```
curl http://api.foo.com/v1/users/12345?active=true
```

POST

POST is used to create a resource. The POST requests are neither idempotent nor safe. Multiple invocations of the POST requests can create multiple resources.

The POST requests should invalidate a cache entry if it exists. Query parameters with the POST requests are not encouraged.

For example, a POST request to create a user can be as follows:

```
curl -X POST   -d'{"name":"John Doe","username":"jdoe",
   "phone":"412-344-5644"}' http://api.foo.com/v1/users
```

PUT

PUT is used to update a resource. PUT is idempotent but not safe. Multiple invocations of the PUT requests should produce the same results by updating the resource.

The PUT requests should invalidate the cache entry if it exists.

For example, a PUT request to update a user can be as follows:

```
curl -X PUT   -d'{ "phone":"413-344-5644"}'
http://api.foo.com/v1/users
```

DELETE

DELETE is used to delete a resource. DELETE is idempotent but not safe. This is idempotent because based on the RFC 2616, the side effects of N > 0 requests is the same as for a single request. This means once the resource is deleted, calling DELETE multiple times will get the same response.

For example, a request to delete a user can be as follows:

```
curl -X DELETE http://foo.api.com/v1/users/1234
```

HEAD

HEAD is similar to the GET request. The difference is that only HTTP headers are returned and no content is returned. HEAD is idempotent and safe.

For example, a request to send a HEAD request with curl is as follows:

```
curl -X HEAD http://foo.api.com/v1/users
```

 It can be useful to send a HEAD request to see if the resource has changed before trying to get a large representation using a GET request.

PUT versus POST

According to RFC, the difference between PUT and POST is in the Request URI. The URI identified by POST defines the entity that will handle the POST request. The URI in the PUT request includes the entity in the request.

So, POST /v1/coffees/orders means to create a new resource and return an identifier to describe the resource. In contrast, PUT /v1/coffees/orders/1234 means to update a resource identified by "1234" if it exists; else create a new order and use the orders/1234 URI to identify it.

 PUT and POST can both be used to create or update methods. The usage of the method depends on the idempotence behavior expected from the method as well as the location of the resource to identify it.

The next section will cover how to identify the different representations of the resource.

Identifying the different representations of the resource

The RESTful resources are abstract entities, which need to be serialized to a representation before they can be communicated to the client. The common representations for a resource can be XML, JSON, HTML, or plain text. A resource can provide the representation to the client based on what the client can handle. A client can specify which language and media type it prefers. This is known as **content negotiation**. *Chapter 2, Resource Design*, covers the content negotiation topic in detail.

Implementing the APIs

Now that we have some idea on designing RESTful resources and associating HTTP verbs to take actions on the resources, we will cover what it takes to implement the APIs and build a RESTful service. This section will cover the following topic:

*   Java API for RESTful Services (JAX-RS)

The Java API for RESTful Services (JAX-RS)

The Java API for RESTful services provides portable APIs for building and developing applications based on the REST architectural style. Using JAX-RS, Java POJOs can be exposed as RESTful web resources, which are independent of the underlying technology and use a simple annotation-based API.

JAX-RS 2.0 is the latest version of the specification and has newer features compared to its predecessor JAX-RS 1.0, especially in the following areas:

*   Bean validation support
*   Client API support
*   Asynchronous invocation support

Jersey is the implementation of JAX-RS specification.

We will cover all these topics in detail in the subsequent chapters. We are demonstrating a simple coffee shop example where you can create a REST resource called CoffeesResource, which can do the following:

*   Give details of the orders placed
*   Create new orders
*   Get details on a specific order

To create a RESTful resource, we begin with a POJO called `CoffeesResource`. An example of a JAX-RS resource is shown as follows:

```
@Path("v1/coffees")
public class CoffeesResource {

    @GET
    @Path("orders")
    @Produces(MediaType.APPLICATION_JSON)
    public List<Coffee> getCoffeeList( ){
        //Implementation goes here

    }
```

1. As shown in the preceding code, we create a small POJO called `CoffeesResource`. We annotate the class with `@Path("v1/coffees")`, which identifies the URI path this class serves requests for.

2. Next, we define a method called `getCoffeeList()`. This method has the following annotations:

    ○   `@GET`: This indicates that the annotated method represents a HTTP GET request.

    ○   `@PATH`: In this example, the GET requests for `v1/coffees/orders` will be handled by this `getCoffeeList()` method.

    ○   `@Produces`: This defines the media types produced by this resource. In our preceding snippet, we define the `MediaType.APPLICATION_JSON` that has the `application/json` value.

3. Another method to create an order is as follows:

```
@POST
@Consumes(MediaType.APPLICATION_JSON)
@Produces(MediaType.APPLICATION_JSON)
@ValidateOnExecution
public Response addCoffee(@Valid Coffee coffee) {
//Implementation goes here
}
```

For the second method of creating an order, we defined a method called `addCoffee()`. This method has the following annotations:

*   `@POST`: This indicates that the annotated method represents the HTTP POST request.

- `@Consumes`: This defines the media types consumed by this resource. In our preceding snippet, we define the `MediaType.APPLICATION_JSON` that has the `application/json` value.

- `@Produces`: This defines the media types produced by this resource. In our preceding snippet, we define the `MediaType.APPLICATION_JSON` that has the `application/json` value.

- `@ValidateOnExecution`: This specifies which methods should have their parameters or return values validated on execution. More details on the `@ValidateOnExecution` and `@Valid` annotations will be covered in *Chapter 3, Security and Traceability*.

Thus, we saw with a simple sample on how easy it is to convert a simple POJO to a REST resource. Now, we will cover the `Application` subclass, which will define the components of a JAX-RS application including the metadata.

The following is the code for a sample `Application` subclass named `CoffeeApplication`:

```
@ApplicationPath("/")
public class CoffeeApplication extends Application {

    @Override
    public Set<Class<?>> getClasses() {
        Set<Class<?>> classes = new HashSet<Class<?>>();
        classes.add(CoffeesResource.class);
        return classes;
    }
}
```

As shown in the preceding code snippet, the `getClasses()` method has been overridden and we add the `CoffeesResource` class to the `Application` subclass. The `Application` classes can be part of `WEB-INF/classes` or `WEB-INF/lib` in the WAR file.

Deploying the RESTful services

Once we have created the resource and added the meta-information to the Application subclass, the next step is to build the WAR file. The WAR file can be deployed on any servlet container.

The source for the samples is available as part of the downloadable bundle with this book, which will have detailed steps to deploy and run the samples.

Test the RESTful services

We can then use the Client API functionality provided by JAX-RS 2.0 to access the resources.

This section will cover the following topics:

- Client API with JAX-RS 2.0

- Accessing RESTful resources using curl, or a browser-based extension called Postman

The Client API with JAX-RS 2.0

JAX-RS 2.0 had newer Client APIs for accessing RESTful resources. The entry point of the client API is `javax.ws.rs.client.Client`.

With the newly introduced Client API in JAX-RS 2.0, the endpoint can be accessed as follows:

```
Client client = ClientFactory.newClient();
WebTarget target = client.target("http://. . ./coffees/orders");
String response = target.request().get(String.class);
```

As shown in the preceding snippet, the default instance of the client is obtained using the `ClientFactory.newClient()` method. Using the `target` method, we create a `WebTarget` object. These target objects are then used to prepare the request by adding the method and the query parameters.

Prior to these APIs, the way we would get access to REST resources was like this:

```
URL url = new URL("http://. . ./coffees/orders");
HttpURLConnection conn = (HttpURLConnection) url.openConnection();
conn.setRequestMethod("GET");
conn.setDoInput(true);
conn.setDoOutput(false);
BufferedReader br = new BufferedReader(new InputStreamReader(conn.
getInputStream()));
String line;
while ((line = br.readLine()) != null) {
    //. . .
}
```

Thus, we can see how there has been an improvement in the JAX-RS 2.0 Client-side API support to avoid using `HTTPURLConnection` and instead use the fluent Client API.

If the request is a POST request:

```
Client client = ClientBuilder.newClient();
Coffee coffee = new Coffee(...);
WebTarget myResource = client.target("http://foo.com/v1/coffees");
myResource.request(MediaType.APPLICATION_XML
  ).post(Entity.xml(coffee), Coffee.class);
```

The `WebTarget.request()` method returns a `javax.ws.rs.client.InvocationBuilder`, which takes a `post()` method to invoke a HTTP POST request. The `post()` method takes an entity from the `Coffee` instance and specifies that the media type is "APPLICATION_XML".

A `MessageBodyReaderWriter` implementation is registered with the client. More on `MessageBodyReader` and `MessageBodyWriter` will be covered in *Chapter 2, Resource Design*.

The following table summarizes some of the main JAX-RS classes/annotations we covered so far.

Name of annotation	Description
javax.ws.rs.Path	This identifies the URI path that the resource serves a method for
javax.ws.rs.ApplicationPath	This is used by a subclass of Application as a base URI for all URIs supplied by the resources in application
javax.ws.rs.Produces	This defines the media type that the resource can produce
javax.ws.rs.Consumes	This defines the media type that the resource can consume
javax.ws.rs.client.Client	This defines the entry point for client requests
javax.ws.rs.client.WebTarget	This defines a resource target identified by the URI

Clients are heavyweight objects that help facilitate the client-side communication infrastructure. It is therefore advised to construct only a small number of client instances in the application, as initialization as well as disposal of a client instance may be a rather expensive operation. Additionally, client instances must be properly closed before being disposed to avoid leaking resources.

Accessing RESTful resources

The following section covers the different ways REST resources can be accessed and tested by clients.

cURL

cURL is a popular command-line tool for testing REST APIs. The cURL library and the cURL command give the user the ability to create a request, put it on the pipe, and explore the response. The following are a few samples of `curl` requests for some basic functions:

curl request	Description
`curl http://api.foo.com/v1/coffees/1`	This is a simple GET request
`curl -H "foo:bar" http://api.foo.com/v1/coffees`	This is an example of a `curl` request for adding request headers using `-H`
`curl -i http://api.foo.com/v1/coffees/1`	This is an example of a `curl` command to view response headers using `-i`
`curl –X POST -d'{"name":"John Doe","username":"jdoe", "phone":"412-344-5644"} http://api.foo.com/v1/users`	This is an example of a `curl` requst for a POST method to create a user

Even though cURL is extremely powerful, it has a lot of options to remember and use. Sometimes, it helps to use a browser-based tool to develop REST API such as Postman or Advanced REST client.

Postman

Postman on the Chrome browser is an excellent tool to test and develop REST API. It has a JSON and XML viewer for rendering the data. It can also allow previewing HTTP 1.1 requests, replay, and organize requests for future use. Postman shares the same environment as the browser and can display browser cookies too.

An advantage of Postman over cURL is that there is a nice user interface for entering parameters so that the user does not need to deal with commands or scripts. Various authorization schemes such as a basic user authentication and digest access authentication are also supported.

The following is a screenshot, which shows how to send queries in Postman:

As shown in the preceding screenshot, we see the Postman application. A simple way to test Postman is to launch the Postman Application from Chrome.

Then, select the HTTP method GET and paste the api.postcodes.io/random/ postcodes URL. (PostCodes is a free, open source service based on geodata.)

You will see a JSON response like this:

```
{
    "status": 200,
    "result": {
        "postcode": "OX1 9SN",
        "quality": 1,
        "eastings": 451316,
        "northings": 206104,
        "country": "England",
        "nhs_ha": "South Central",
        "admin_county": "Oxfordshire",
        "admin_district": "Oxford",
        "admin_ward": "Carfax",
    ...}
}
```

Downloading the example code

You can download the example code files for all Packt books you have purchased from your account at http://www.packtpub.com. If you purchased this book elsewhere, you can visit http://www.packtpub. com/support and register to have the files e-mailed directly to you.

On the left pane of the preceding screenshot are different queries, which have been added to a collection like getting all the coffee orders, getting a specific order, creating orders, and so on based on testing the various samples in this book. You can create custom collections of queries similarly.

 For more details, check `http://www.getpostman.com/`.

Other tools

Here are some additional tools, which can be very useful when working with REST resources.

Advanced REST Client

Advanced REST Client is another Chrome extension based on Google WebToolkit, which allows the user to test and develop REST API.

JSONLint

JSONLint is a simple online validator that ensures the JSON is valid. When sending JSON data as part of requests, it is useful to validate if the format of the data conforms to the JSON specification. In such cases, the client can validate the input using JSONLint. For more details, check `http://jsonlint.com/`.

Best practices when designing resources

The following section highlights some of the best practices when designing RESTful resources:

- The API developer should use nouns to understand and navigate through resources and verbs with the HTTP method, for example, the `/user/1234/books` is better than `/user/1234/getBook` URI.

- Use associations in the URIs to identify subresources. For example, to get the authors for book 5678, for user 1234, use the following `/user/1234/books/5678/authors` URI.

- For specific variations, use query parameters. For example, to get all the books with 10 reviews, use `/user/1234/books?reviews_counts=10`.

- Allow partial responses as part of query parameters if possible. An example of this case is to get only the name and age of a user, the client can specify, ?fields as a query parameter and specify the list of fields that should be sent by the server in the response using the `/users/1234?fields=name,age` URI.

- Have defaults for the output format for the response in case the client does not specify which format it is interested in. Most API developers choose to send JSON as the default response mime type.

- Have camelCase or use _ for attribute names.

- Support a standard API for counts, for example `users/1234/books/count`, in case of collections so that the client can get an idea of how many objects can be expected in the response.

  This will also help the client with pagination queries. More details on pagination will be covered in *Chapter 5*, *Advanced Design Principles*.

- Support a pretty printing option, `users/1234?pretty_print`. Also, it is a good practice to not cache queries with a pretty print query parameter.

- Avoid chattiness by being as verbose as possible in the response. This is because if the server does not provide enough details in the response, the client needs to make more calls to get additional details. That is a waste of network resources as well as counts against the client's rate limits. More details on rate limiting are covered in *Chapter 5*, *Advanced Design Principles*.

Recommended reading

The following links may be useful to review for more details:

- **RFC 2616**: `http://www.w3.org/Protocols/rfc2616/rfc2616-sec3.html`
- **Richardson Maturity Model**: `http://www.crummy.com/writing/speaking/2008-QCon/act3.html`
- **Jersey implementation of JAX-RS**: `https://jersey.java.net/`
- **InspectB.in**: `http://inspectb.in/`
- **Postman**: `http://www.getpostman.com/`
- **Advanced REST Client**: `https://code.google.com/p/chrome-rest-client/`

Summary

In this chapter, we covered the fundamentals of REST, CRUD API, and how to design RESTful resources. We worked with JAX-RS 2.0-based annotations that can represent HTTP methods and Client APIs that can be used to target the resources. Additionally, we iterated the best practices when designing RESTful services.

The next chapter will dig deeper into the concepts covered here. We will also cover topics such as content negotiation, entity providers in JAX-RS 2.0, error handling, versioning schemes, and response codes in REST. We will look into techniques the server can use to send responses to the client using Streaming or Chunking.

2
Resource Design

Chapter 1, REST – Where It Begins, covered the basics of REST as well as best practices while designing RESTful resources. This chapter continues the discussion with an understanding of request response patterns, how to deal with different representations of resources, what are the different strategies when versioning API, and how standard HTTP codes can be used with REST responses. Subsections of this chapter will cover the following topics:

- REST response patterns
- Content negotiation
- Entity providers and different representations
- API versioning
- Response codes and REST patterns

We will also cover custom entity providers for serializing and de-serializing request and response entities as well as other approaches such as streaming and chunking.

REST response patterns

In the earlier chapter, we saw how we can work with domain-related data to create readable URIs, use HTTP methods for different CRUD functionality, and transfer data to and fro from the clients and server using standardized MIME types and HTTP response codes.

The following is a diagram that shows standard REST request/response patterns:

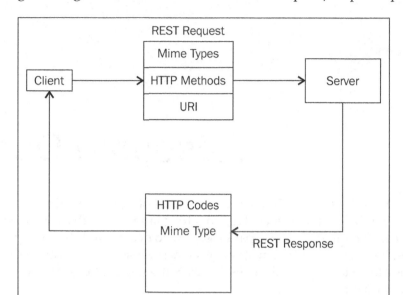

As seen from the preceding diagram, the client makes a REST request, which consists of standard HTTP methods, MIME types, and the URI to target. The server processes the request and sends back a response, which comprises standard HTTP response codes and MIME types. We covered the HTTP methods and how to use JAX-RS annotations earlier. Also, we enumerated the best practices for designing Resource URIs. In this chapter, we will cover the commonly used HTTP response codes as well as how to handle the different MIME types.

Content negotiation

Content negotiation means allowing different representations of a resource in the same URI so that clients can make a choice on what suits them best.

> *"HTTP has provisions for several mechanisms for "content negotiation" - the process of selecting the best representation for a given response when there are multiple representations available."*
>
> *– RFC 2616, Fielding et al.*

There are different patterns for content negotiation. These are as follows:

- Using HTTP headers
- Using URL patterns

Content negotiation using HTTP headers

When the client sends requests to create or update a resource, there is some form of payload that should be transferred from the client to the endpoint. Also, when a response is generated, a payload can be sent back to the client. These payloads are handled by HTTP request and response entities, which are sent as part of the HTTP messages body.

Entities are sent via a request, usually for HTTP POST and PUT methods, or they are returned in a response for the HTTP methods. The Content-Type HTTP header is used to indicate the MIME type of the entity being sent by the server. Common examples of content types are "text/plain", "application/xml", "text/html", "application/json", "image/gif", and "image/jpeg".

A client can make a request to the server and specify what media types it can handle and what is its order of preference as part of the "Accept" HTTP header. The client can also specify in what language it wants the response as part of the "Accept-Language" header to be. If no Accept header is present in the request, the server can send the representation it chooses.

The JAX-RS specification provides standard annotations to support content negotiation. These are javax.ws.rs.Produces and javax.ws.rs.Consumes annotations. The following snippet shows an example of the @Produces annotation in a resource method:

```
@GET
@Path("orders")
@Produces(MediaType.APPLICATION_JSON)
public List<Coffee> getCoffeeList(){
    return CoffeeService.getCoffeeList();

}
```

The getCoffeeList() method returns a list of coffees and is annotated with @Produces(MediaType.APPLICATION_JSON). The @Produces annotation is used to specify which MIME types the resource can send back to the client and match it up to the client's Accept header.

This method will produce a response as shown:

```
X-Powered-By: Servlet/3.1 JSP/2.3 (GlassFish Server Open Source
Edition  4.0  Java/Oracle Corporation/1.7)
Server: GlassFish Server Open Source Edition  4.0
Content-Type: application/json
Date: Thu, 31 Jul 2014 15:25:17 GMT
Content-Length: 268
{
    "coffees": [
        {
            "Id": 10,
            "Name": "Cappuchino",
            "Price": 3.82,
            "Type": "Iced",
            "Size": "Medium"
        },
        {
            "Id": 11,
            "Name": "Americano",
            "Price": 3.42,
            "Type": "Brewed",
            "Size": "Large"
        }
    ]
}
```

In a resource, if no methods are able to produce the MIME type requested by a client request, the JAX-RS runtime sends back an HTTP 406 Not Acceptable error.

The following snippet shows a resource method annotated with the @Consumes annotation:

```
@POST
@Consumes(MediaType.APPLICATION_JSON)
@Produces(MediaType.APPLICATION_JSON)
public Response addCoffee(Coffee coffee) {
    // Implementation here
}
```

The @Consumes annotation specifies which media types the resource can consume. When a client makes a request, JAX-RS finds all the methods that will match the path, and it will then invoke the method based on the content type sent by the client.

If a resource is unable to consume the MIME type of a client request, the JAX-RS runtime sends back an HTTP 415 ("Unsupported Media Type") error.

Multiple MIME types can be specified in the `@Produces` or `@Consumes` annotation as `@Produces(MediaType.APPLICATION_JSON, MediaType.APPLICATION_XML)`.

Along with the support for static content negotiation, JAX-RS also contains runtime content negotiation support using the `javax.ws.rs.core.Variant` class and the `javax.ws.rs.core.Request` objects. A `Variant` object in a JAX-RS specification is a combination of media types, content-language, and content encoding as well as ETags, last-modified headers, and other preconditions. The `Variant` object defines the resource representation that is supported by the server. The `Variant.VariantListBuilder` class is used to build a list of representation variants.

The following code snippet shows how to create a list of resource representation variants:

```
List<Variant>  variants = Variant.mediatypes("application/xml",
    "application/json").build();
```

The code snippet calls the build method of the `VariantListBuilder` class. The `Request.selectVariant` method takes a list of `Variant` objects and chooses the one based on the client's `Accept` header, as shown in the following snippet:

```
@GET
public Response getCoffee(@Context Request r) {
    List<Variant> vs = ...;
    Variant v = r.selectVariant(vs);
    if (v == null) {
        return Response.notAcceptable(vs).build();
    } else {
        Coffee coffee = ..//select the representation based on v
        return Response.ok(coffee, v);
    }
}
```

Content negotiation based on URL patterns

Another approach for content negotiation adopted by some APIs is to send the resource representation based on the extension of a resource in the URL. For example, a client can ask for details using `http://foo.api.com/v2/library/books.xml` or `http://foo.api.com/v2/library/books.json`. The server has different methods, which can handle the two URIs. However, both of these are representations of the same resource.

```
@Path("/v1/books/")
public class BookResource {
```

```
@Path("{resourceID}.xml")
@GET
public Response getBookInXML(@PathParam("resourceID") String
    resourceID) {
    //Return Response with entity in XML
        }

@Path("{resourceID}.json")
@GET
public Response getBookInJSON(@PathParam("resourceID") String
    resourceID) {
    //Return Response with entity in JSON
}
}
```

As you can see in the preceding snippet, there are two methods defined: getBookInXML() and getBookInJSON(), and the response is returned based on the path of the URL.

 It is a good practice to use the HTTP content negotiation Accept header. Using headers for content negotiation provides a clear separation of IT concerns from business. The other advantage with using the Accept header for content negotiation is that there is only one resource method for all the different representations.

The following section covers how to serialize and de-serialize a resource to and from the different representations respectively using entity providers in JAX-RS.

Entity providers and different representations

In the previous examples, we passed literal parameters picked from a URI path fragment as well as from the request's query parameters to the resource method. However, there are cases when we want to pass a payload in the request body, for example a POST request. JAX-RS provides two interfaces that can be used: one for handling the inbound entity representation-to-Java de-serialization known as javax.ws.rs.ext.MessageBodyReader, and the other one for handling the outbound entity Java-to-representation serialization known as javax.ws.rs.ext.MessageBodyWriter.

`MessageBodyReader` de-serializes entities from the message body representation into Java classes. `MessageBodyWriter` serializes a Java class to a specific representation format.

The following table shows the methods that need to be implemented:

Method of MessageBodyReader	Description
`isReadable()`	This is used to check if the `MessageBodyReader` class can support conversion from a stream to Java type
`readFrom()`	This is used to read a type from the `InputStream` class

As shown in the table, the `isReadable()` method of the `MessageBodyReader` implementation class is called to check if `MessageBodyReader` can handle the specified input. When the `readFrom()` method of the `MessageBodyReader` class is called, it can convert an input stream to a Java POJO.

The following table shows the methods of `MessageBodyWriter` that must be implemented along with a short description of each of its methods:

Method of MessageBodyWriter	Description
`isWritable()`	This is used to check if the `MessageBodyWriter` class can support the conversion from the specified Java type
`getSize()`	This is used to check the length of bytes if the size is known or -1
`writeTo()`	This is used to write from a type to the stream

The `isWritable()` method of the `MessageBodyWriter` implementation class is called to check if the `MessageBodyWriter` class can handle the specified input. When the `writeTo()` method of `MessageBodyWriter` is called, it can convert a Java POJO to the output stream. The samples in the download bundle of this book show how to use `MessageBodyReader` and `MessageBodyWriter`.

However, there are lightweight implementations such as the `StreamingOutput` and `ChunkingOutput` classes, and the following sections will cover how Jersey implementation of JAX-RS already has support for basic formats such as text, JSON, and XML.

StreamingOutput

The `javax.ws.rs.core.StreamingOutput` class is a callback that can be implemented to send the entity in the response when the application wants to stream the output. The `StreamingOutput` class is a lightweight alternative to the `javax.ws.rs.ext.MessageBodyWriter` class.

The following is a sample code that shows how to use `StreamingOutput` as part of the response:

```
@GET
@Produces(MediaType.TEXT_PLAIN)
@Path("/orders/{id}")
public Response streamExample(@PathParam("id") int id) {
    final Coffee coffee = CoffeeService.getCoffee(id);
    StreamingOutput stream = new StreamingOutput() {
        @Override
        public void write(OutputStream os) throws IOException,
                WebApplicationException {
            Writer writer = new BufferedWriter(new
              OutputStreamWriter(os));
            writer.write(coffee.toString());
            writer.flush();
        }
    };
    return Response.ok(stream).build();
}
```

As shown in the preceding snippet, the `write()` method of the `StreamingOutput` class has been overridden to write to the output stream. `StreamingOutput` is useful in case of streaming binary data in a streaming fashion. For more details, have a look at the samples code that are available as part of the download bundle.

ChunkedOutput

With Jersey implementation of JAX-RS, the server can use the `org.glassfish.jersey.server.ChunkedOutput` class to immediately send a response to a client in chunks as soon as they become available, without waiting for the other chunks to become available too. The `size` object's value of -1 is sent in the `Content-Length` header of the response to indicate that the response will be chunked. On the client side, it will know that the response will be chunked, so it reads each chunk of the response separately and processes it and waits for more chunks to come on the same connection. The server keeps on sending response chunks until it closes the connection after sending the last chunk and the response processing is finished.

The following is an example code to show the use of ChunkedOutput:

```
@GET
@Produces(MediaType.TEXT_PLAIN)
@Path("/orders/{id}/chunk")
public ChunkedOutput<String> chunkExample(final @PathParam("id")
int id) {
    final ChunkedOutput<String> output = new
ChunkedOutput<String>(String.class);

    new Thread() {
        @Override
        public void run() {
            try {
                output.write("foo");
                output.write("bar");
                output.write("test");
            } catch (IOException e) {
                e.printStackTrace();
            } finally {
                try {
                    output.close();
                } catch (IOException e) {
                    e.printStackTrace();
                }
            }
        }
    }.start();
    return output;

    }
}
```

As shown in the snippet, the chunkExample method returns a ChunkedOutput object.

On the client side, org.glassfish.jersey.client.ChunkedInput can be used to receive messages in "typed" chunks. This data type is useful for consuming partial responses from large or continuous data input streams. The following snippet shows how the client can read from a ChunkedInput class:

```
ChunkedInput<String> input = target().path("..").request().get(new Gen
ericType<ChunkedInput<String>>() {
        });
while ((chunk = chunkedInput.read()) != null) {
    //Do something
}
```

Differences between ChunkedOutput and StreamingOutput

ChunkedOutput is an internal class provided by Jersey. It lets the server send *chunks* of data without closing the client connection. It uses a series of convenient calls to the ChunkedOutput.write methods that take POJO and media type input and then use the JAX-RS MessageBodyWriter class to convert the POJO to bytes. ChunkedOutput writes are non-blocking.

StreamingOutput is a low-level JAX-RS API that works with bytes directly. The server has to implement StreamingOutput, and its write(OutputStream) method will be invoked only once by JAX-RS runtime, and the call is blocking.

Jersey and JSON support

Jersey provides support for the following approaches when working with a JSON representation.

POJO-based JSON binding support

POJO-based JSON binding support is very generic and allows mapping from any Java object to JSON. This is done via a Jackson org.codehaus.jackson.map. ObjectMapper instance. For example, to read a JSON in a Coffee object, we use the following:

```
ObjectMapper objectMapper = new ObjectMapper();
Coffee coffee = objectMapper.readValue(jsonData, Coffee.class);
```

For more details, check https://jersey.java.net/documentation/1.18/json. html.

JAXB-based JSON binding support

JAXB-based JSON binding support is useful if the resource can produce and consume XML or JSON. To implement this, you can annotate a simple POJO with @XMLRootElement, as shown in the following code:

```
@XMLRootElement
public class Coffee {
    private String type;
    private String size;
}
```

Using the preceding JAXB bean to produce the JSON data format from the resource method is then as simple as using the following:

```
@GET
@Produces("application/json")
public Coffee getCoffee() {
    //Implementation goes here
}
```

The `Produces` annotation will take care of converting into a JSON representation of the `Coffee` resource.

Low-level JSON parsing and processing support

This is best used to get fine-grained control over the JSON format using `JSONArray` and `JSONObject` to create the JSON representation. The advantage here is that the application developer will gain full control over the JSON format produced and consumed. The following is an example code to use `JSONArray`:

```
JsonObject myObject = Json.createObjectBuilder()
        .add("name", "Mocha")
        .add("size", "Large")
        .build();
```

On the other hand, dealing with the data model objects will probably be a bit more complex. For example, the following code shows how the pull parsing programming model works with JSONParser:

```
JsonParser parser = Json.createParser(...)
Event event = parser.next(); // START_OBJECT
event = parser.next(); //END OBJECT
```

The next section covers the topic of how to version the API so that it can evolve over a period of time as well as how to ensure the basic functionality of a client application does not break with API versioning changes on the server side.

API versioning

For the evolution of the application, the URI design should have some constraints to identify the version. It is hard to foresee all the resources, which will change during the life of the application. The goal with API versioning is to define the resource endpoints and the addressing schemes and associate a version with them. The API developers must ensure the HTTP verbs' semantics and status codes should continue to work without human intervention as the version changes. Over the life span of the application, the version will evolve, and the APIs may need to be deprecated. Requests to older versions of the API can be redirected to the latest code path or there can be appropriate error codes that indicate the API is obsolete.

There can be different approaches to version APIs. These are as follows:

- Specify the version in the URI itself
- Specify the version in the request query parameter
- Specify the version in the `Accept` header

All of these could work fine. The next section covers the approaches in detail and highlights the advantages and disadvantages of each.

Version in the URI approach

In this approach, the version is part of the URI for the resource exposed by the server.

For example, in the following URL, there is a "v2" version exposed as part of the path to the resource:

```
http://api.foo.com/v2/coffees/1234
```

Additionally, API developers can provide a path, which defaults to the latest version of the API. Thus, the following request URIs should behave identically:

- `http://api.foo.com/coffees/1234`
- `http://api.foo.com/v2/coffees/1234`

This indicates v2 is the latest API version. If the clients point to the older versions, they should be informed to use the newer versions by using the following HTTP code for redirection:

- `301 Moved permanently`: This indicates that the resource with a requested URI is moved permanently to another URI. This status code can be used to indicate an old or unsupported API version, informing the API client that a versioned resource URI has been replaced by a resource permalink.

- `302 Found`: This indicates that the requested resource is temporarily located at another location, while the requested URI might still be supported.

Version as part of the request query parameter

The other way to use API versioning could be to send the version in the request parameter. The resource method can choose the flow of code based on the version, which is sent with the request. For example, in the `http://api.foo.com/coffees/1234?version=v2` URL, v2 has been specified as part of the query parameter `?version=v2`.

The disadvantage with this format is that the responses may not be cached. Additionally, the source code for the resource implementation will have different flows based on the version in the query parameter, which is not very intuitive or maintainable.

> More details on the best practices of caching will be covered in *Chapter 4*, *Designing for Performance*.

In contrast, if the URI contains the version, it is cleaner and more readable. Also, there could be a standardized lifespan for a version of URI, after which all the requests to older versions get redirected to the latest version.

> Facebook, Twitter, and Stripe API all use versions as part of the URI. The Facebook API makes a version unusable two years after the date on which the subsequent version is released. If a client makes an unversioned call, the server will default to the oldest available version of the Facebook API.
>
> The Twitter API provides six months to completely transition from v1.0 to v1.1.
>
> More details on these APIs will be found in the *Appendix*.

Specifying the version in the Accept header

Some APIs prefer to put version as part of the `Accept` header. For example, take a look at the following code snippet:

```
Accept: application/vnd.foo-v1+json
```

In the preceding snippet, `vnd` stands for vendor-specific MIME type. This removes the version for the URL and is preferred by some API developers.

The GitHub API recommends you send an `Accept` header explicitly, as shown:

`Accept: application/vnd.github.v3+json`

For more details, check `https://developer.github.com/v3/media/`.

The next section covers what the standard HTTP response codes that should be sent to the client are.

Response codes and REST patterns

HTTP provides standardized response codes that can be returned for every request. The following table summarizes the REST response patterns based on CRUD API. There are subtle differences based on the operation used as well as whether the content is sent or not as part of the response:

Group	Response code	Description
Success 2XX	200 OK	This can be used for the `create`, `update`, or `delete` operations with `PUT`, `POST`, or `DELETE`. This returns content as part of the response.
	201 Created	This can be used when creating a resource with `PUT`. This must contain the `Location` header of the resource.
	204 No Content	This can be used for the `DELETE`, `POST`, or `PUT` operation. No content is returned as part of the response.
	202 Accepted	This sends a response later as processing has not been completed as yet. This is used for asynchronous operations. This should also return a `Location` header, which can specify where the client can monitor for the request.
Redirectional 3XX	301 Permanent	This can be used to show that all requests are directed to a new location.
	302 Found	This can be used to show the resource already exists and is valid.
Client Errors 4XX	401 Unauthorized	This is used to show the request can't be processed based on the credentials.

Group	Response code	Description
	404 Not Found	This is used to show the resource is not found. It is a good practice to return a 404 Not Found error to the unauthenticated requests to prevent information leaks.
	406 Not Acceptable	This can be used when the resource cannot produce the MIME type specified by the client. This happens when the MIME type specified in the Accept header does not match any media type in the resource method/class annotated with @Produces.
	415 Unsupported Media Type	This can be used when the client sends a media type that cannot be consumed by the resource. This happens when the MIME type specified in the Content-Type header does not match any media type in the resource method/class annotated with @Consumes.
Server Errors 5XX	500 Internal Server error	This internal server error is a generic message when no specific details are available.
	503 Service Unavailable	This can be used when the server is under maintenance or too busy to handle requests.

JAX-RS defines a javax.ws.rs.core.Response class, which has static methods to create an instance using javax.ws.rs.core.Response.ResponseBuilder:

```
@POST
Response addCoffee(...) {
    Coffee coffee = ...
    URI coffeeId = UriBuilder.fromResource(Coffee.class)...
    return Response.created(coffeeId).build();
}
```

The preceding code snippet shows a method addCoffee(), which returns a 201 Created response using the Response.created() method. For more details on other response methods, check https://jersey.java.net/apidocs/latest/jersey/javax/ws/rs/core/Response.html.

Recommended reading

- `https://jersey.java.net/documentation/latest/representations.html`: Jersey documentation for content negotiation

- `http://docs.jboss.org/resteasy/docs/2.2.1.GA/userguide/html/JAX-RS_Content_Negotiation.html`: RESTEasy and URL-based content negotiation

- `https://dev.twitter.com/docs/api/1.1/overview`: Twitter REST API and versioning strategy

- `https://developers.facebook.com/docs/apps/versions`: The Facebook API and versioning

Summary

We covered topics such as content negotiation, API versioning, and REST response codes in this chapter. One of the primary takeaways from this chapter was to understand how important it is to support various representations of the same resource so that the client can choose the right one for their case. We covered differences between streaming and chunking output and how they can be used as lightweight options with custom entity providers such as `MessageBodyReader` and `MessageBodyWriter`. We saw case studies of companies that use versioning in their solutions as well as best practices and design principles scattered throughout the various topics.

The next chapter will cover advanced details such as security, traceability, and validation in REST programming models.

3
Security and Traceability

In the era of open platforms, developers can build apps, which can be easily and quickly decoupled from the platform's business cycle. This API-based architecture enables agile development, easier adoption, prevalence, and scale and integration with applications within and outside the enterprise. One of the most important considerations for the apps is dealing with security. The developers building apps should not be concerned with the user's credentials. Additionally, there can be other clients consuming the REST services including but not limited to browsers and mobile applications to other services. The clients can be acting on behalf of other users and must be authorized to perform actions for them without the user having to share his credentials for a username and password. This is where the OAuth 2.0 specification comes into the picture.

Another important aspect to consider when building distributed applications is traceability, which will involve logging the data related to requests for debugging purposes in an environment encompassing multiple micro services, which can be geographically distributed and deal with thousands of requests. Requests to the REST resources and status codes must be logged to help debug issues in production and can also serve as an audit trail. This chapter will cover advanced details in security and traceability in REST programming models. The topics covered are as follows:

- Logging REST APIs
- Exception handling with RESTful services
- Validation patterns
- Federated identity
    - SAML 2.0
    - OAuth 2.0
    - OpenID Connect

This chapter will conclude with what it takes to work with the various building blocks for scalable, highly performing RESTful services.

Logging REST APIs

Complex distributed applications can introduce many points of failure. Problems are hard to find and fix, thus delaying incident response and creating costly escalations. Application developers and administrators may not have direct access to the machine data they need.

Logging is a very important aspect of building RESTful services, especially in the case of debugging production issues in distributed nodes running various micro services. It helps to link events or transactions between the various components that make an application or a business service. A complete sequence of logs can help replay the course of events that occurred in a production system. Additionally, logs can help index, aggregate, slice the data, analyze the patterns of requests coming in, and provide a lot of potentially helpful information.

The following code covers how to write a simple logging filter, which can be integrated with the REST resources. The filter will log request-related data such as timestamp, query string, and inputs:

```java
@WebFilter(filterName = "LoggingFilter",
        urlPatterns = {"/*"}
)
public class LoggingFilter implements Filter {
    static final Logger logger =
       Logger.getLogger(LoggingFilter.class);
    @Override
    public void doFilter(ServletRequest servletRequest,
      ServletResponse servletResponse,
           FilterChain filterChain) throws IOException,
             ServletException {

        HttpServletRequest httpServletRequest =
           (HttpServletRequest) servletRequest;

logger.info("request"
  +httpServletRequest.getPathInfo().toString());
        filterChain.doFilter(servletRequest, servletResponse);

    }
```

The `LoggingFilter` class is a simple filter that implements a `javax.servlet.Filter` interface. The logger will log all messages with the request path and inputs. The sample uses Apache Log4j to set up logging.

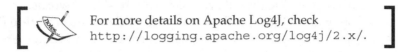

For more details on Apache Log4J, check `http://logging.apache.org/log4j/2.x/`.

These logs can then be collected and mined from a distributed log server application, for example, Splunk (`http://www.splunk.com/`), which can give the developer information and root causes analysis for outages or performance issues in production. An example in our coffee shop analogy could be that there was a problem processing a coffee order. If the request details were logged in a distributed log server application such as Splunk, the developer can query based on the time, and see what the client tried to send and why the request failed.

The next section will cover numerous best practices to keep in mind when logging REST API.

Best practices for the logging REST API

In a large-scale distributed environment, the log data may be the only information that is available to the developer for debugging issues. Auditing and logging, if done right, can help tremendously in figuring such production issues and replaying the sequence of steps that occurred before an issue. The following sections list a few best practices for logging to understand system behavior and reasoning for performance and other issues.

Including a detailed consistent pattern across service logs

It is a good practice for a logging pattern to at least include the following:

- Date and current time
- Logging level
- The name of the thread
- The simple logger name
- The detailed message

Obfuscating sensitive data

It is very important to mask or obfuscate sensitive data in production logs to protect the risk of compromising confidential and critical customer information. Password obfuscators can be used in the logging filter, which will mask passwords, credit card numbers, and so on from the logs. **Personally identifiable information** (PII is information that can be used by itself or along with some other information to identify a person. Examples of PII can be a person's name, e-mail, credit card number, and so on. Data representing PII should be masked using various techniques such as substitution, shuffling, encryption, and other techniques.

 For more details, check `http://en.wikipedia.org/wiki/Data_masking`.

Identifying the caller or the initiator as part of the logs

It is a good practice to identify the initiator of the call in the logs. The API may be called by a variety of clients, for example, mobile, the Web, or other services. Adding a way to identify the caller may help debug issues in case the problems are specific to a client.

Do not log payloads by default

Have a configurable option to log payloads so that by default no payload is logged. This will ensure, for resources dealing with sensitive data, the payloads do not get logged in the default case.

Identifying meta-information related to the request

Every request should have some details on how long it took to execute the request, the status of the request, and the size of the request. This will help to identify latency issues as well as any other performance issues that may come up with large messages.

Tying the logging system with a monitoring system

Ensure the data from the logs can also be tied to a monitoring system, which can collect data related to SLA metrics and other statistics in the background.

Case studies of logging frameworks in distributed environments in various platforms

Facebook has developed a homegrown solution called Scribe, which is a server for aggregating streaming log data. This can handle the large number of requests per day across servers distributed globally. The servers send data, which can be processed, diagnosed, indexed, summarized, or aggregated. Scribe is designed to scale to a very large number of nodes. It is designed to be robust to survive network and node failures. There is a scribe server running on every node in the system. It is configured to aggregate messages and sends them to a central scribe server in larger groups. If the central scribe server goes down, messages are written to a file by the local scribe server on the local disk and sends them when the central server recovers. For more details, check `https://github.com/facebookarchive/scribe`.

Dapper is Google's tracing system, which samples data from the thousands of requests and provides sufficient information to trace data. Traces are collected in local logfiles and then pulled in Google's BigTable database. Google has found out that sampling sufficient information for common cases can help trace the details. For more details, check `http://research.google.com/pubs/pub36356.html`.

The next section will cover how to validate REST API requests and/or response entities.

Validating RESTful services

When exposing REST- or HTTP-based service APIs, it is important to validate that the API behaves correctly and that the exposed data format is structured in an expected manner. For example, it is important to validate an input to a RESTful service, such as e-mails sent as part of the request body, must conform to the standards, certain values in the payload must be present, the zip code must follow a particular format, and so on. This can be done by validations with RESTful services.

JAX-RS supports the Bean Validation to verify JAX-RS resource classes. This support consists of:

- Adding constraint annotations to resource method parameters
- Ensuring entity data is valid when the entity is passed in as a parameter

The following is a code snippet of a `CoffeesResource` class, which contains the `@Valid` annotation:

```
@POST
@Consumes(MediaType.APPLICATION_JSON)
@Produces(MediaType.APPLICATION_JSON)
@ValidateOnExecution
public Response addCoffee(@Valid Coffee coffee) {
    ...
        }
```

The `javax.validation.executable.ValidateOnExecution` annotation can help specify which method or constructor should have their parameters and return values validated on execution. The `javax.validation.Valid` annotation on the request body will ensure the `Coffee` object will conform to the rules as specified in the POJO.

The following is the snippet of the `Coffee` POJO:

```
@XmlRootElement
public class Coffee {

    @VerifyValue(Type.class)
    private String type;

    @VerifyValue(Size.class)
    private String size;

    @NotNull
    private String name;
    // getters and setters
}
```

The field name has a `javax.validation.constrains.NotNull` annotation, which enforces that the name of the coffee in the order cannot be null. Similarly, we have defined custom annotations in the sample, which will verify the type and size and check if the values in the request body follow the right format.

For example, `Size` can be either of the following values as shown: `Small`, `Medium`, `Large`, or `ExtraLarge`:

```
public enum Size {
    Small("S"), Medium("M"), Large("L"), ExtraLarge("XL");
    private String value;
}
```

The `@VerifyValue(Size.class)` annotation is a custom annotation defined in the downloadable sample.

Validation exception handling and response codes

The following table provides a quick summary of the type of response codes when various validation-related exceptions are thrown. The type of error code depends on the exception thrown as well as whether the validation performed is on the request or the response of the HTTP method.

HTTP Response code returned	Type of exception
500 Internal Server Error	This error code is returned when `javax.validation.ValidationException` or any subclass of `ValidationException` including `ConstraintValidationException` is thrown while validating a method return type
400 Error	When `ConstraintViolationException` is thrown in all other cases for validating method

The next section covers how the API developers can throw application-specific exceptions and map HTTP error codes based on the exceptions.

Error handling with RESTful services

When building RESTful APIs, it is necessary to throw application-specific exceptions and provide specific HTTP responses containing the details of these exceptions. The following section covers how to deal with user-defined exceptions and map them to HTTP responses and status codes. The `javax.ws.rs.ext.ExceptionMapper` classes are custom, application provided, components that catch thrown application exceptions and write specific HTTP responses. Exception mapper classes are annotated with the `@Provider` annotation.

The following snippets show how to build your custom exception mapper:

```
@GET
@Produces(MediaType.APPLICATION_JSON)
@Path("/orders/{id}")
public Response getCoffee(@PathParam("id") int id) {
    Coffee coffee =  CoffeeService.getCoffee(id);
    if (coffee == null)
```

```
        throw new CoffeeNotFoundException("No coffee found for
            order " + id);
        return Response.ok(coffee).type(MediaType.APPLICATION_JSON_
TYPE).build();
    }
```

As shown in the preceding code snippet, the `getCoffees()` method returns a `Coffee` object with the ID specified in the path parameter. If no coffee is found with the ID specified, the code throws a `CoffeeNotFoundException`.

The following is the code of an `ExceptionMapper` class implementation:

```
@Provider
public class MyExceptionMapper implements ExceptionMapper<Exception> {

    public Response toResponse(Exception e) {
        ResourceError resourceError = new ResourceError();

        String error = "Service encountered an internal error";
        if (e instanceof CoffeeNotFoundException) {
            resourceError.setCode(
              Response.Status.NOT_FOUND.getStatusCode());
            resourceError.setMessage(e.getMessage());

            return Response.status(
              Response.Status.NOT_FOUND).entity(resourceError)
                    .type(MediaType.APPLICATION_JSON_TYPE)
                    .build();
        }
        return Response.status(503).entity(
          resourceError).type(MediaType.APPLICATION_JSON_TYPE)
                .build();
    }
}
```

The preceding code shows an implementation of `ExceptionMapper` whose `toResponse()` method has been overridden. The code checks if the exception thrown is an instance of `CoffeeNotFoundException`, then returns a response whose entity is of the type `ResourceError`.

The `ResourceError` class is a POJO annotated with `@XMLRootElement` and sent as part of the response:

```
@XmlRootElement
public class ResourceError {

    private int code;
    private String message;
    //getters and setters
...}
```

You can run the sample as part of the downloadable bundle and the output is as follows:

```
HTTP/1.1 404 Not Found
X-Powered-By: Servlet/3.1 JSP/2.3 (GlassFish Server Open Source
Edition  4.0  Java/Oracle Corporation/1.7)
Server: GlassFish Server Open Source Edition 4.0
Content-Type: application/json
Content-Length: 54

{"code":404,"message":"No coffee found for order 100"}
```

Authentication and authorization

In the past, organizations needed a way to unify the authentication for users in an enterprise. Single sign-on is a solution to keep one repository for usernames and passwords that can be used across the different applications in an enterprise.

With the evolution of service-oriented architectures, organizations needed a way so that the partners and other services could use the APIs and there needed to be a way to simplify the sign-on process across the various applications and platforms. The need grew with the generation of social media with various platforms opening up, the APIs and an ecosystem built with a myriad of applications, and a multitude of devices using the platforms such as Twitter, Facebook, and LinkedIn.

Thus, it has become increasingly important to decouple the authentication and authorization functions from the consumer application. Also, it is not mandatory for every application to be aware of the user's credentials. The following section will cover SAML 2.0 and OAuth 2.0 for authorization as part of the federated identities effort to simplify sign-on and increase security.

Subsections will enumerate over the following topics:

* SAML
* OAuth
* Refresh tokens versus Access tokens
* Jersey and OAuth 2.0
* When to use SAML or OAuth?
* OpenID Connect

What is authentication?

Authentication is the process of establishing and communicating that the person operating a browser or native app is who he/she claims to be.

SAML

Security Assertion Markup Language (**SAML**) is a standard that encompasses profiles, bindings, and constructs to achieve **Single sign-on** (**SSO**), federation, and identity management.

The SAML 2.0 spec provides a web browser SSO profile, which defines how single sign-on can be achieved for web applications. It defines three roles:

* **Principal**: This is where the user is typically looking to verify his or her identity
* **Identity provider** (**IdP**): This is the entity that is capable of verifying the identity of the end user
* **Service provider** (**SP**): This is the entity looking to use the identity provider to verify the identity of the end user

The following flow shows a simple example of SAML. Say, an employee wants to access the corporate travel website. The corporate travel application will request the identity provider the employee is associated with to verify his identity and then take actions for him.

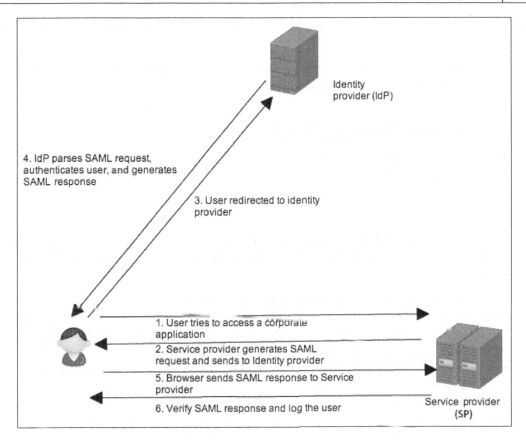

The flow is explained as follows:

1. The user accesses a corporate application, say, travel application.

2. The travel application will generate a SAML request and redirects the user to the employer's **identity provider (IdP)**.

3. The user is redirected to the employer's identity provider to obtain a SAML authentication assertion.

4. The IdP parses the SAML request, authenticates the user, and generates a SAML response.

5. The browser sends the SAML response to the travel application.

6. On receiving the access token, the corporate travel app is then able to access the web resource by passing the token in the header of the HTTP request. The access token acts as a session token that encapsulates the fact that the travel app is acting on behalf of the user.

SAML has binding specifications for web browsers, SSO, SOAP, and WS-Security but no formal binding for the REST API.

The next section covers OAuth, which has been widely used by platforms such as Twitter, Facebook, and Google for authorization.

What is authorization?

Authorization is the process of checking whether the requestor has permissions to perform the requested operation.

OAuth

OAuth stands for **open authorization** and provides a way for a user to authorize an application to access their account-related data without giving out their username and password.

Traditionally in client/server authentication, the client uses its credentials to access resources on the server. The server does not care if the request comes from the client or if the client is requesting the resource for some other entity. The entity can be another application or another person and thus the client is not accessing its own resource but that of another user. Anyone requesting access to a resource that is protected and requires authentication must be authorized to do so by the resource owner. OAuth is a way to open up the REST APIs for companies such as Twitter, Facebook, Google+, GitHub, and so on, and the myriad of third-party applications built on top of them. OAuth 2.0 completely relies on SSL.

The number of legs in an OAuth request refers to the number of parties involved. A flow where there is client, server, and resource owner indicates 3-legged OAuth. When the client is acting on behalf of itself, it is known as 2-legged OAuth.

OAuth achieves this functionality with the help of access tokens. Access tokens are like valet keys that give access to limited functionality for a limited period of time. Tokens have a limited lifespan from hours to a few days. The following diagram shows the flow of OAuth:

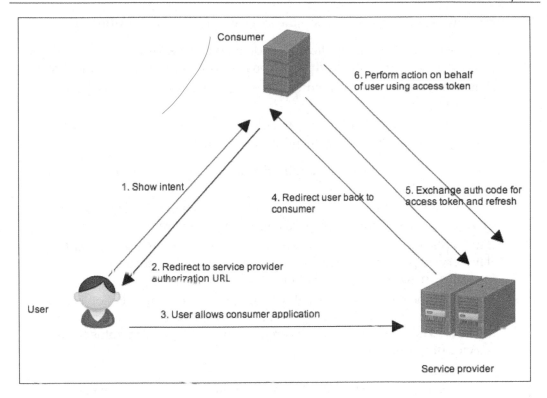

The preceding diagram shows the authorization code grant flow.

In this example, a user has his photos on a service provider site, say, Flickr. Now, the user needs to call a print service to print his photos, for example, Snapfish, which is a consumer application. Instead of the user sharing his username and password to the consumer application, the user can use OAuth to allow the print service to access his photos for a limited period of time.

So in our example, we have three roles as described:

- **User or resource owner**: The user is the resource owner who wants to print his photos
- **Consumer application or client**: This is the print service application, which will act on behalf of the user
- **Service provider or server**: The service provider is the resource server that will store the user's photos

With this example in mind, we can see the steps involved in the OAuth dance:

1. User wants to allow an application to do a task on his behalf. In our example, the task is to print photos, which are on a server using a consumer application.

2. The consumer application redirects the user to the service provider's authorization URL.

   Here, the provider displays a web page asking the user if they can grant the application access to read and update their data.

3. The user agrees to grant the application access by the print service consumer application.

4. The service provider redirects the user back to the application (via the redirect URI), passing an authorization code as a parameter.

5. The application exchanges the authorization code for an access grant. The service provider issues the access grant to the application. The grant includes an access token and a refresh token.

6. Now that the connection is established, the consumer application can now obtain a reference to the service API and invoke the provider on behalf of the user. Thus, the print service can now access the user's photos from the service provider's site.

> The advantage of OAuth is that a compromised application will not create much havoc as access tokens are used instead of actual credentials. The SAML bearer flow is actually very similar to the classic OAuth 3-leg flow covered earlier. However, instead of redirecting the user's browser to the authorization server, the service provider works with the identity provider to get a simple authentication assertion. The service provider application swaps a SAML bearer assertion for the user instead of exchanging an authorization code.

Differences between OAuth 2.0 and OAuth 1.0

OAuth 2.0 specification clearly lays out how to use OAuth entirely inside a browser using JavaScript that has no way to securely store a token. This also explains at a high level how to use OAuth on a mobile phone or even on a device that has no web browser at all, covering interactions to *apps* and *native applications* on both smartphones and traditional computing devices, in addition to websites.

OAuth 2.0 defines the following three types of profiles:

- Web application (In this case, the client password is stored on the server, and access tokens are used.)

- Web browser client (In this case, the OAuth credentials are not trusted; some providers won't issue a client secret. An example is JavaScript in the browser.)

- Native application (In this case, access tokens or refresh tokens that are generated can provide an acceptable level of protection. An example includes mobile applications.)

OAuth 2.0 does not require encryption and uses HTTPS not HMAC. Additionally, OAuth 2.0 allows limiting the lifetime of an access token.

An authorization grant

An authorization grant is a credential representing the resource owner or the user's authorization, which allows a client to access its protected resources to obtain an access token. The OAuth 2.0 specification defines four grant types as follows:

- The authorization code grant
- The implicit grant
- The resource owner password credentials grant
- The client credentials grant

Additionally, OAuth 2.0 also defines an extensibility mechanism for defining additional types.

Refresh tokens versus access tokens

Refresh tokens are credentials used to obtain access tokens. Refresh tokens are used to obtain the access token when the current access token becomes invalid or expires. Issuing a refresh token is optional at the discretion of the server.

Unlike access tokens, refresh tokens are intended for use only with authorization servers and are never sent to resource servers to access a resource.

Jersey and OAuth 2.0

Even though OAuth 2.0 is widely used by various enterprises, OAuth 2.0 RFC is a framework to build solutions on top of it. There are numerous gray areas in the RFC where the specification leaves it to the implementer. There were indecisions in areas where there is no required token type, no agreement on the token expiration, or no specific guidance on the token size.

 Read this page for more details:
`http://hueniverse.com/2012/07/26/oauth-2-0-and-the-road-to-hell/`

Currently, Jersey support for OAuth 2.0 is only on the client side. OAuth 2.0 specification defines many extension points and it is up to service providers to implement these details. Additionally, OAuth 2.0 defines more than one authorization flow. The Authorization Code Grant Flow is the flow currently supported by Jersey and none of the other flows are supported. For more details, check `https://jersey.java.net/documentation/latest/security.html`.

Best practices for OAuth in the REST API

The following section lists some of the best practices that can be followed by service providers implementing OAuth 2.0.

Limiting the lifetime for an access token

The protocol parameter `expires_in` allows an authorization server to limit the lifetime of an access token and to pass this information to the client. This mechanism can be used to issue short-living tokens.

Support providing refresh tokens in the authorization server

A refresh token can be sent along with a short lifetime access token to grant longer access to resources without involving user authorization. This offers an advantage where resource servers and authorization servers may not be the same entity. For example, in a distributed environment, the refresh token is always exchanged at the authorization server.

Using SSL and encryption

OAuth 2.0 heavily relies on HTTPS. This will make the framework simpler but less secure.

The following table provides a quick summary of when to use SAML and when to use OAuth.

Scenario	SAML	OAuth
If one of the parties is an enterprise	Use SAML	
If the application needs to provide temporary access to some resources		Use OAuth
If the application needs a custom identity provider	Use SAML	
If the application has mobile devices accessing it		Use OAuth
If the application has no restrictions on the transport, for example, SOAP and JMS	Use SAML	

OpenID Connect

There is work going on at the OpenID foundation with OpenID Connect. OpenID Connect is a simple REST- and JSON-based interoperable protocol built on top of OAuth 2.0. It is simpler than SAML, easy to maintain, and covers the various security levels from social networks to business applications to highly secure government applications. OpenID Connect and OAuth are the future for authentication and authorization. For more details, check `http://openid.net/connect/`.

Case studies of companies using OAuth 2.0 and OpenID Connect

Google+ Sign-In is built on the OAuth 2.0 and OpenID Connect protocols. It supports over-the-air installs, social features, and a sign-in widget on top of standardized OpenID Connect sign-in flows.

The next section will summarize some of the various components that we have covered so far when building RESTful services.

REST architecture components

The following section will cover the various components that must be considered when building RESTful APIs. All of these will be covered in various sections of this book. We will also cover best practices for each pitfall to avoid when designing and developing the REST API. The REST architecture components are shown in the following diagram:

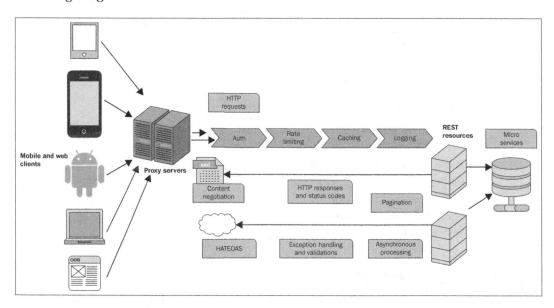

As seen from the preceding diagram, REST services can be consumed from a variety of clients and applications running on different platforms and devices such as mobile devices and web browsers.

These requests are sent through a proxy server. The REST architectural components in the diagram can be chained one after the other as shown in the preceding diagram. For example, there can be a filter chain, consisting of the **Auth**, **Rate limiting**, **Caching**, and **Logging** related filters. This will take care of authenticating the user, checking if the requests from the client are within rate limits, then a caching filter that can check if the request can be served from the cache respectively. This can be followed by a logging filter, which can log the details of the request.

On the response side, there can be **Pagination**, to ensure the server sends a subset of results. Also, the server can do **Asynchronous processing**, thus improving responsiveness and scale. There can be links in the response, which deals with HATEOAS.

These are some of the REST architectural components we have covered so far:

- HTTP requests to use the REST API with HTTP verbs for the uniform interface constraint
- Content negotiation to select a representation for a response when there are multiple representations available
- Logging to provide traceability to analyze and debug issues
- Exception handling to send application-specific exceptions with HTTP codes
- Authentication and authorization with OAuth 2.0 to give access control to other applications and to take actions without the user having to send their credentials
- Validation to send back detailed messages with error codes to the client as well as validations for the inputs received in the request

The next few chapters will focus on advanced topics as well as best practices for the following blocks. We will provide code snippets to show how to implement these with JAX-RS.

- Rate limiting to ensure the server is not burdened with too many requests from a single client
- Caching to improve application responsiveness
- Asynchronous processing so that the server can asynchronously send back the responses to the client
- Micro services that comprise breaking up a monolithic service into fine-grained services
- HATEOAS to improve usability, understandability, and navigability by returning a list of links in the response
- Pagination to allow clients to specify items in a dataset that they are interested in

We will also cover how major platforms such as Facebook, Google, GitHub, and PayPal have approached each of these solutions in their REST API.

Recommended reading

The following links can be useful to get additional information related to the topics in this chapter:

- `https://developers.google.com/oauthplayground/`: Google OAuth playground to create and test signed requests

- `http://hueniverse.com/2012/07/26/oauth-2-0-and-the-road-to-hell/`: OAuth 2.0 and road to hell

- `https://developers.google.com/accounts/docs/OAuth2Login`: Google Accounts Authentication and Authorization

- `https://github.com/facebookarchive/scribe`: Scribe log server for Facebook

- `http://static.googleusercontent.com/media/research.google.com/en/us/pubs/archive/36356.pdf`: Google Dapper large-scale distributed tracing architecture

Summary

This chapter started off with a brief introduction to logging RESTful APIs and the key principles were to recognize the importance of logging requests and best practices for logging including security compliance. We learned how to validate JAX-RS 2.0 resources using Bean Validation. In this chapter, we also saw how to write generic exception mappers for application-specific cases.

We covered how federated identities are a necessity in the current era of interconnected hybrid systems, protocols, and devices. We covered SAML and OAuth 2.0 similarities between SAML and 3-legged OAuth as well as best practices for OAuth.

The next chapter will walk through topics such as caching patterns and asynchronous REST API to improve performance and scalability, followed by a closer look at how to perform partial updates with HTTP Patch and the newer JSON Patch.

4
Designing for Performance

REST is an architectural style confirming to the web architecture design and needs to be properly designed and implemented so that it allows you to take advantage of the scalable web. This chapter covers advanced design principles related to performance that every developer must know when building RESTful services.

Topics covered in this chapter include the following:

- Caching principles
- Asynchronous and long-running jobs in REST
- HTTP PATCH and partial updates

We will elaborate on the different HTTP cache headers and learn how to send conditional requests to see whether the new content or the cached content needs to be returned. We will then show with samples how to use JAX-RS to implement caching.

Additionally, we will cover how the Facebook API uses ETags for caching. Next, we will walk through asynchronous request response processing with JAX-RS and best practices. Finally, we will cover HTTP PATCH method and learn how to implement partial updates and common practices around partial updates.

Different snippets of code are included in the chapter, but complete samples that show these snippets in action are included as part of this book's source code download bundle.

Caching principles

In this section, we will cover the different programming principles when designing RESTful services. One of the areas we will cover is caching. Caching involves storing response information related to the requests in a temporary storage for a specific period of time. This ensures the server is not burdened with processing those requests in future when the responses can be fulfilled from the cache.

The cache entries can be invalidated after a specific time interval. The cache entries can also be invalidated when the objects, which are in the cache, change, for example, when some API modifies or deletes a resource.

There are many benefits to caching. Caching helps to reduce **latency** and improve application responsiveness. It helps in reducing the number of requests the server has to deal with and thus the server is able to handle more requests, and the clients will get responses quicker.

Generally, assets such as images, JavaScript files, and stylesheets can all be cached fairly heavily. Also, it is advisable to cache responses, which may require intensive computation on the backend.

Caching details

The following section covers the topics related to caching. The key to making caching work effectively is to use HTTP caching headers that specify how long a resource is valid and when it was last changed.

Types of caching headers

The next section covers the types of caching headers followed by examples of each type of caching header. The following are the types of headers:

- Strong caching headers
- Weak caching headers

Strong caching headers

The strong caching headers specify for how long a cached resource is valid and the browser does not need to send any more `GET` requests till that period. `Expires` and `Cache-Control max-age` are strong caching headers.

Weak caching headers

The weak caching headers help the browser decide if it needs to fetch an item from the cache by issuing a conditional GET request. Last-Modified and ETag are examples of weak caching headers.

Expires and Cache-Control – max-age

The Expires and Cache-Control headers specify the time period during which the browser can use the cached resource without checking for a newer version. The newer resource will not be fetched until the expiry date or maximum age specified is reached if these headers are set. The Expires header takes a date after which the resource becomes invalid. Instead of specifying a date, the max-age attribute mentions how long the resource is valid after it is downloaded.

The Cache-Control header and directives

In **HTTP 1.1**, the Cache-Control header specifies the resource caching behavior as well as the maximum age the resource can be cached. The following table shows the different directives of the Cache-Control header:

Directive	Meaning
private	When this directive is used, the browser can cache the object, but proxies and content delivery networks cannot
public	When this directive is used, an object can be cached by browser, proxies, and content delivery networks
no-cache	When this directive is used, an object will not be cached
no-store	When this is used, an object can be cached in memory but should not be stored on disk
max-age	This denotes the time for which the resource is valid

Here is an example of a response with the Cache-Control HTTP/1.1 header in a response:

```
HTTP/1.1 200 OK Content-Type: application/json
Cache-Control: private, max-age=86400
Last-Modified: Thur, 01 Apr 2014 11:30 PST
```

The preceding response has a `Cache-Control` header with directives as `private` and `max-age` set to 24 hours or 86400 seconds.

Once a resource is invalid based on the `max-age` or `Expires` header, the client can request the resource again or send a conditional GET request that gets the resource only if it has changed. This can be achieved by the weaker caching headers: the `Last-Modified` and ETag headers as shown in the next section.

Last-Modified and ETag

These headers enable the browser to check if the resource has changed since the last GET request. In the `Last-Modified` header, there is a date associated with the modification of the resource. In the ETag header, there can be any value that uniquely identifies a resource (like a hash). However, these headers allow the browser to efficiently update its cached resources by issuing conditional GET requests. Conditional GET requests will return the full response only if the resource has changed at the server. This ensures conditional GET requests will have lower latency than full GET requests.

The Cache-Control header and the REST API

The following code shows how to add the `Cache-Control` header to a JAX-RS response. The sample is available as part of the book's downloadable source bundle.

```
@Path("v1/coffees")
public class CoffeesResource {

    @GET
    @Path("{order}")
    @Produces(MediaType.APPLICATION_XML)
    @NotNull(message = "Coffee does not exist for the order id
      requested")
    public Response getCoffee(@PathParam("order") int order) {
        Coffee coffee = CoffeeService.getCoffee(order);
        CacheControl cacheControl = new CacheControl();
        cacheControl.setMaxAge(3600);
        cacheControl.setPrivate(true);
        Response.ResponseBuilder responseBuilder =
          Response.ok(coffee);
        responseBuilder.cacheControl(cacheControl);
        return responseBuilder.build();


    }
```

JAX-RS has a `javax.ws.rs.core.Cache-Control` class, which is an abstraction for the `HTTP/1.1 Cache-Control` header. The `setMaxAge()` method on the `cacheControl` object corresponds to the `max-age` directive and `setPrivate(true)` corresponds to the `private` directive. The response is built using the `responseBuilder.build()` method. The `cacheControl` object is added to the `Response` object that is returned by the `getCoffee()` method.

The following is the response with headers produced by this application:

```
curl -i http://localhost:8080/caching/v1/coffees/1
HTTP/1.1 200 OK
X-Powered-By: Servlet/3.1 JSP/2.3 (GlassFish Server Open Source
Edition  4.0  Java/Oracle Corporation/1.7)
Server: GlassFish Server Open Source Edition  4.0
Cache-Control: private, no-transform, max-age=3600
Content-Type: application/xml
Date: Thu, 03 Apr 2014 06:07:14 GMT
Content-Length: 143

<?xml version="1.0" encoding="UTF-8" standalone="yes"?>
<coffee>
<name>Mocha</name>
<order>1</order>
<size>Small</size>
<type>Chocolate</type>
</coffee>
```

ETags

HTTP defines a powerful caching mechanism that includes the following headers:

- The `ETag` header
- The `If-Modified-Since` header
- The `304 Not Modified` response code

How ETags work

The following section digs into some basics of how ETags work. The following diagram gives a better picture of this:

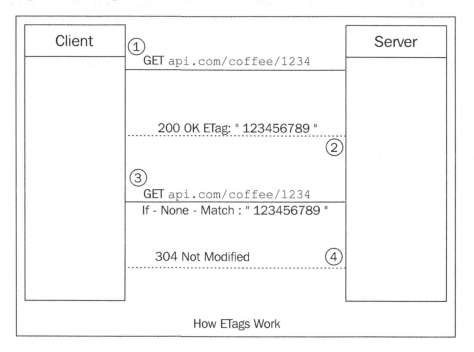

How ETags Work

Let's have a look at each of the processes related to ETags:

1. The client sends a GET request to the `http://api.com/coffee/1234` REST resource.

2. The server sends back a **200 OK** with an **ETag** value, for example, **"123456789"**.

3. After some time, the client sends another GET request to `api.com/coffee/1234` REST resource along with the `If-None-Match: "123456789"` header.

4. The server checks if the resource MD5 hash has not been modified, then sends a `304 Not-Modified` response with no response body.

If the resource had changed, a 200 OK would be sent as the response. Additionally, as part of the response, a new ETag is sent by the server.

The ETag header and the REST API

The following code shows how to add the ETag header to the JAX-RS response:

```
@GET
@Path("/etag/{order}")
@Produces(MediaType.APPLICATION_JSON)
@NotNull(message = "Coffee does not exist for the order id
    requested")
public Response getCoffeeWithEtag(@PathParam("order")
    int order,

                              @Context Request request
) {
    Coffee coffee = CoffeeService.getCoffee(order);
    EntityTag et = new EntityTag(
            "123456789");
    Response.ResponseBuilder responseBuilder   =
      request.evaluatePreconditions(et);
    if (responseBuilder != null) {
        responseBuilder.build();
    }
    responseBuilder = Response.ok(coffee);
    return responseBuilder.tag(et).build();
```

In the preceding snippet of code, the instance of `javax.ws.core.EntityTag` object is created by using a hash of the resource, which for simplicity, we have "123456789".

The `request,evalautePreconditions` method checks for the value of the `EntityTag` et object. If the preconditions are met, it returns a response with 200 OK.

The `EntityTag` object, et, is then sent with the response, which is returned by the `getCoffeeWithETag` method. For more details, please refer to the sample available as part of the source bundle for the book.

Types of ETags

A strongly validating ETag match indicates that the content of the two resources is byte-for-byte identical and that all other entity fields (such as Content-Language) are also unchanged.

A weakly validating ETag match only indicates that the two resources are semantically equivalent, and that cached copies can be used.

Caching helps reduce the number of requests made by the client. It also helps in reducing the number of complete responses saving bandwidth and computational time with the conditional GET requests and ETags, IF-None-Match headers, and 304-Not Modified response.

 It is a good practice to specify either Expires or Cache-Control max-age along with one of the two Last-Modified and ETag headers in the HTTP response. Sending both Expires and Cache-Control max-age is redundant. Similarly, sending both Last-Modified and ETag is redundant.

The Facebook REST API and ETags

The Facebook Marketing API supports ETags on the Graph API. When the consumer makes a Graph API call, the response header includes an ETag with a value that is the hash of the data returned in the API call. Next time the consumer makes the same API call, he can include the If-None-Match request header with the ETag value saved from the first step. If the data has not changed, the response status code will be 304 -Not Modified and no data is returned.

If the data on the server side has changed since the last query, the data is returned as usual with a new ETag. This new value of ETag can be used for subsequent calls. For more details, check http://developers.facebook.com.

RESTEasy and caching

RESTEasy is a JBoss project that provides various frameworks to help build RESTful web services and RESTful Java applications. RESTEasy can run in any servlet container, but has a tighter integration with the JBoss Application Server.

RESTEasy provides an extension to JAX-RS that allows setting Cache-Control headers on a successful GET request automatically.

It also provides a server-side, local, in-memory cache that can sit in front of the JAX-RS services. It automatically caches marshalled responses from HTTP GET JAX-RS invocations if the JAX-RS resource method sets a Cache-Control header.

When a HTTP GET request arrives, the RESTEasy server cache will check to see if the URI is stored in the cache. If it does, it returns the already marshalled response without invoking the JAX-RS method.

For more information, check `http://www.jboss.org/resteasy`.

Tips when caching on the server side

Invalidate the cache entry for a PUT or a POST request. Do not cache a request that has a query parameter, as once the query parameter value changes the cached response from the server may not be valid.

Asynchronous and long-running jobs in REST

A common pattern in developing RESTful API is to deal with asynchronous and long-running jobs. API developers need to create resources that might take a considerable amount of time. They cannot have the clients wait on the API to finish.

Consider placing an order for a coffee at a coffee shop. The order details are stored in a queue and when the barista is free, he processes your order. Till then you get a receipt acknowledging your order but the actual coffee arrives later.

Asynchronous resource processing works on the same principles. Asynchronous resources mean the resources cannot be created immediately. Maybe it will be placed inside a task/message queue that will handle the actual creation of the resource or something similar.

Consider the following request to order a small coffee in our sample:

```
POST v1/coffees/order HTTP 1.1 with body
<coffee>
  <size> SMALL</coffee>
  <name>EXPRESSO</name>
  <price>3.50</price>
<coffee>
```

The response can be sent back as the following:

```
HTTP/1.1 202 Accepted
Location: /order/12345
```

The response sends back a `202 Accepted` header. The `Location` header can provide details about the coffee resource.

Asynchronous request and response processing

The asynchronous processing is included in both client- and server-side APIs of JAX-RS 2.0 to facilitate asynchronous interaction between client and server components. The following list shows the new interfaces and classes added to support this feature on the server and the client side:

- Server side:
    - ○ AsyncResponse: This is an injectable JAX-RS asynchronous response that provides means for asynchronous server-side response processing
    - ○ @Suspended: The @Suspended annotation instructs the container that the HTTP request processing should happen in a secondary thread
    - ○ CompletionCallback: This is a request-processing callback that receives request-processing completion events
    - ○ ConnectionCallback: This is an asynchronous request-processing lifecycle callback that receives connection-related asynchronous response lifecycle events

- Client side:
    - ○ InvocationCallback: This is a callback that can be implemented to receive the asynchronous processing events from the invocation processing
    - ○ Future: This allows the client to poll for completion of the asynchronous operation or to block and wait for it

The Future interface introduced in Java SE 5 provides two different mechanism to get the result of an asynchronous operation: first by invoking the Future.get (...) variants that blocks until the result is available or a timeout occurs, and the second way is to check for completion by invoking the isDone() and isCancelled(), which are Boolean methods that return the current status of Future. For more details, check http://docs.oracle.com/javase/1.5.0/docs/api/java/util/concurrent/Future.html.

The following diagram shows the asynchronous request/response processing in JAX-RS:

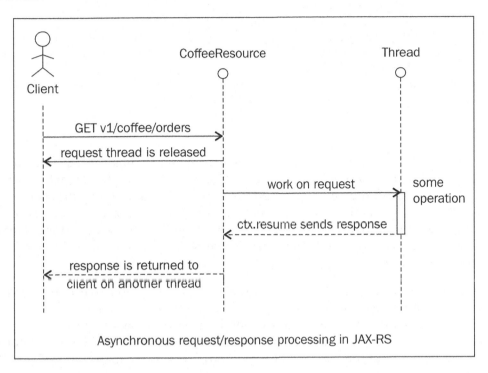

Asynchronous request/response processing in JAX-RS

The client makes a request for an asynchronous method on `CoffeeResource`. The `CoffeeResource` class creates a new thread, which can do some intensive operation and then send back the response. Meanwhile, the request thread is released and can handle other requests. When the thread working on the operation finishes the processing, it returns the response to the client.

The following sample code shows how an asynchronous resource can be developed using JAX-RS 2.0 API:

```
@Path("/coffees")
@Stateless
public class CoffeeResource {
  @Context private ExecutionContext ctx;
  @GET @Produce("application/json")
  @Asynchronous
  public void order() {
```

```
        Executors.newSingleThreadExecutor().submit( new Runnable()
          {
        public void run() {
            Thread.sleep(10000);
            ctx.resume("Hello async world! Coffee Order is
              1234");
          } });
ctx.suspend();
return;
  }
}
```

The `CoffeesResource` class is a stateless session bean, which has a method called `order()`. This method is annotated with the `@Asynchronous` annotation, which will work in the fire-and-forget manner. When the resource is requested by the client through the `order()` method's resource path, a new thread is spawned to work on preparing the request's response. The thread is submitted to the executor for execution and the thread processing the client request is released (via `ctx.suspend`) to process other incoming requests.

When the worker thread, created to prepare the response, is done with preparing the response, it invokes the `ctx.resume` method, which lets the container know the response is ready to be sent back to the client. If the `ctx.resume` method is invoked before the `ctx.suspend` method (the worker thread has prepared the result before the execution reaching the `ctx.suspend` method), the suspension is ignored and the result will be sent to the client.

The same functionality can be achieved using the `@Suspended` annotation that is shown in the following snippet:

```
@Path("/coffees")
@Stateless
public class CoffeeResource {
@GET @Produce("application/json")
@Asynchronous
  public void order(@Suspended AsyncResponse ar) {
    final String result = prepareResponse();
    ar.resume(result)
  }
}
```

Using the @Suspended annotation is cleaner as this does not involve the use of the ExecutionContext variable to instruct the container to suspend and then resume the communication thread when the worker thread, aka the prepareResponse() method in this case, is finished. The client code to consume the asynchronous resource can use the callback mechanism or polling at the code level. The following code shows how to use polling via the Future interface:

```
Future<Coffee> future = client.target("/coffees")
                    .request()
                    .async()
                    .get(Coffee.class);
try {
    Coffee coffee = future.get(30, TimeUnit.SECONDS);
} catch (TimeoutException ex) {
  System.err.println("Timeout occurred");
}
```

The code begins with forming the request to the Coffee resource. It uses the javax.ws.rs.client.Client instance to call the target() method, which creates a javax.ws.rs.client.WebTarget instance for the Coffee resource. The Future.get(...) method blocks until the response is back from the server or the 30 seconds timeout is reached.

Another API for the asynchronous client is to use the javax.ws.rs.client. InvocationCallback instance, which is a callback that can be implemented to get asynchronous events from the invocation. For more details, check https://jax-rs-spec.java.net/nonav/2.0/apidocs/javax/ws/rs/ client/InvocationCallback.html.

Asynchronous resources best practices

The following section lists the best practices when working with asynchronous RESTful resources.

Sending a 202 Accepted message

For asynchronous requests/responses, the API should send back a 202 Accepted message, in case the request is valid and the resource may be available in time, even if it is a few seconds. 202 Accepted means the request has been accepted for processing and the resource will be available shortly. The 202 Accepted message should specify the Location header, which can be used by the client to know where the resource will be available once it is created. The API should not send back a 201 Created message if the response is not available immediately.

Setting expiration for objects in the queue

The API developer should expire the objects after a certain amount of time in the queue. This ensures queue objects do not accumulate over time and are purged periodically.

Using message queues to handle tasks asynchronously

The API developer should consider using message queuing for asynchronous operations so that the messages are placed in the queue until a receiver receives them. **Advanced Messaging Queuing Protocol (AMQP)** is a standard that enables reliable and secure routing, queuing, publishing, and subscribing of messages. For more details, check Advanced Message Queuing Protocol at `http://en.wikipedia.org/wiki/Advanced_Message_Queuing_Protocol`.

For example, when an asynchronous resource method is invoked, use message queuing to send messages and handle different tasks based on messages and events asynchronously.

In our sample, if a coffee order is placed, a message can be sent using RabbitMQ (`http://www.rabbitmq.com/`) to trigger the `COMPLETED` event. Once the order is completed, the details can be moved to an inventory system.

The next section covers another important detail for RESTful services for doing partial updates.

HTTP PATCH and partial updates

A common problem for API developers is to implement partial updates. This can happen when the client sends a request that must change just one part of a resource's state. For example, imagine that there is a JSON representation of your `Coffee` resource that looks like the following code snippet:

```
{
  "id": 1,
  "name": "Mocha"
  "size": "Small",
  "type": "Latte",
  "status":"PROCESSING"
}
```

Once the order is completed, the status needs to be changed from `"PROCESSING"` to `"COMPLETED"`.

In an RPC-style API, this could be handled by adding a method as follows:

```
GET myservice/rpc/coffeeOrder/setOrderStatus?
  completed=true&coffeeId=1234
```

In the REST case using the PUT method, all the data like this needs to be sent, which will waste bandwidth and memory.

```
PUT /coffee/orders/1234
{
 "id": 1,
 "name": "Mocha"
 "size": "Small",
 "type": "Latte",
 "status": "COMPLETED"
}
```

To avoid sending the whole data for a minor update, another solution is to use PATCH to do a partial update:

```
PATCH /coffee/orders/1234
{
"status": "COMPLETED"
}
```

However, not all web servers and client will provide support for PATCH, so people have been supporting both partial updates with POST and PUT:

```
POST /coffee/orders/1234
{
"status": "COMPLETED"
}
```

Partial updates with PUT:

```
PUT /coffee/orders/1234
{
"status": "COMPLETED"
}
```

To summarize, using either PUT or POST for partial updates are both acceptable. The Facebook API uses POST to update partial resources. Using partial PUT would be more consistent with how we implement RESTful resources and methods as CRUD operations.

To implement support for the PATCH method, here is how to add an annotation in JAX-RS:

```
@Target({ElementType.METHOD})
  @Retention(RetentionPolicy.RUNTIME)
  @HttpMethod("PATCH")
  public @interface PATCH {
}
```

The preceding snippet shows how to associate the annotation of javax.ws.rs. HTTPMethod with the name "PATCH". Once this annotation is created, then the @PATCH annotation can be used on any JAX-RS resource method.

JSON Patch

JSON Patch is part of RFC 6902. It is a standard designed to allow performing operations on JSON documents. JSON Patch can work with the HTTP PATCH method. It is useful to provide partial updates to JSON documents. The media type "application/json-patch+json" is used to identify such patch documents.

It takes the following members:

- op: This identifies the operation to be performed on the document. The acceptable values are "add", "replace", "move", "remove", "copy", or "test". Any other value is an error.

- path: This is the JSON pointer that represents the location in the JSON document.

- value: This denotes the value to be replaced in the JSON document.

The move operation takes a "from" member, which identifies the location in the target document to move the value from.

Here is an example of a JSON Patch document sent in a HTTP PATCH request:

```
PATCH /coffee/orders/1234 HTTP/1.1
Host: api.foo.com
Content-Length: 100
Content-Type: application/json-patch


[
  {"op":"replace", "path": "/status", "value": "COMPLETED"}
]
```

The preceding request shows how JSON Patch can be used to replace the status of a coffee order identified by resource `coffee/orders/1234` .The operation, that is, `"op"` in the preceding snippet, is `"replace"`, which sets the value `"COMPLETED"` to the status object in the JSON representation.

The JSON Patch is very useful for single-page applications, real-time collaboration, offline data changes, and can also be used in applications that need to make small updates in large documents. For more details, check `http://jsonpatchjs.com/`, which is an implementation of `JSON Patch.(RFC 6902)` and `JSON Pointer.(RFC 6901)` under the MIT License.

Recommended reading

The following section lists some of the online resources that are related to the topics covered in this chapter and may be useful for review:

- RESTEasy: `http://resteasy.jboss.org/`
- Couchbase: `http://www.couchbase.com/`
- Facebook Graph API Explorer: `https://developers.facebook.com/`
- RabbitMQ: `https://www.rabbitmq.com/`
- JSON Patch RFC 6902: `http://tools.ietf.org/html/rfc6902`
- JSON Pointer RFC 6901: `http://tools.ietf.org/html/rfc6901`

Summary

This chapter covered some serious ground introducing fundamental concepts of caching, demonstrating the different HTTP caching headers such as `Cache-Control`, `Expires`, and so on. We also saw how headers work and how ETags and `Last-Modified` headers work for conditional `GET` requests that can improve performance. We covered best practices for caching, how RESTEasy supports server-side caching, and how Facebook API uses ETags. This chapter addressed asynchronous RESTful resources and best practices when working with an asynchronous API. We covered HTTP Patch and partial updates along with JSON Patch (RFC 6902).

The next chapter will deal with advanced topics that every developer building RESTful services should know related to commonly used patterns and best practices in areas of rate limiting, response pagination, and internationalization of REST resources. It will also cover additional topics such as HATEOAS, REST, and their extensibility.

5
Advanced Design Principles

This chapter covers advanced design principles that every developer must know when designing RESTful services. It also provides pragmatic insights that give the developer enough information to build complex applications with REST API.

This chapter will cover the following topics:

- Rate-limiting patterns
- Response pagination
- Internationalization and localization
- REST pluggability and extensibility
- Additional topics for REST API developers

Different snippets of code are included in the chapter, but the complete samples that show these snippets in action are included as part of the book's source code download bundle.

As we have done with the prior chapters, we'll attempt to cover the minimal level of detail required to empower the reader with a solid general understanding of inherently complex topics, while also providing enough of a technical drill-down so that the reader will be able to immediately get to work easily.

Rate-limiting patterns

Rate limiting involves restricting the number of requests that can be made by a client. A client can be identified based on the access token it uses for the request as covered in *Chapter 3*, *Security and Traceability*. Another way the client can be identified is the IP address of the client.

To prevent abuse of the server, APIs must enforce throttling or rate-limiting techniques. Based on the client, the rate-limiting application can decide whether to allow the request to go through or not.

The server can decide what the natural rate limit per client should be, say for example, 500 requests per hour. The client makes a request to the server via an API call. The server checks if the request count is within the limit. If the request count is within the limit, the request goes through and the count is increased for the client. If the client request count exceeds the limit, the server can throw a 429 error.

The server can optionally include a `Retry-After` header, which indicates how long the client should wait before it can send the next request.

Every request from an application can be subjected to two different throttles: those with an access token and those without an access token. The quota of requests made by an application with an access token can vary from an application without an access token.

Here are the details of the `HTTP 429 Too Many Requests` error code.

429 Too Many Requests (RFC 6585)

The user has sent too many requests in a given amount of time. This is intended for use with rate-limiting schemes.

The response for a `429 Too Many Requests` error may include a `Retry-After` header, indicating how long the client needs to wait before making a new request. The following is an example code snippet:

```
HTTP/1.1 429 Too Many Requests
Content-Type: text/html
Retry-After: 3600
 <html>
      <head>
   <title>Too Many Requests</title>
   </head>
 <body>
```

```
<h1>Too many Requests</h1>
    <p>100 requests per hour to this Web site per
        logged in use allowed.</p>
</body>
</html>
```

The preceding example of an HTTP response sets a `Retry-After` header to 3600 seconds to indicate when the client can retry later. Additionally, servers can send an `X-RateLimit-Remaining` header that can indicate how many requests are pending for this client.

Now that we have some ideas on what rate limiting is and how the rate-limiting error and `Retry-After` and `X-RateLimit-Remaining` headers work, let's get down to code with JAX-RS.

The following code in the *The project's layout* section shows how to implement a simple rate-limiting filter in JAX-RS.

The project's layout

The project's directory layout follows the standard Maven structure, which is briefly explained in the following table. This sample produces a WAR file, which can be deployed on any Java EE 7-compliant application server such as GlassFish 4.0.

This sample demonstrates a simple coffee shop service where clients can query for a particular order they placed.

Source code	Description
src/main/java	This directory contains all the sources required by the coffee shop application

The `CoffeeResource` class is a simple JAX-RS resource, shown as follows:

```
@Path("v1/coffees")
public class CoffeesResource {
    @GET
    @Path("{order}")
    @Produces(MediaType.APPLICATION_XML)
    @NotNull(message="Coffee does not exist for the order id
      requested")
    public Coffee getCoffee(@PathParam("order") int order) {
        return CoffeeService.getCoffee(order);
    }
}
```

The project has a `CoffeeResource` class that is used to get details about the coffee orders. The `getCoffee` method returns a `Coffee` object that contains the details of the order.

To enforce rate limiting, we will add a `RateLimiter` class that is a simple servlet filter as shown in the following diagram.

The `RateLimiter` class will check the IP address of the client and check if the number of requests that are made by the client exceeds the limit or not. The following diagram depicts the rate-limiting functionality covered by the sample in detail:

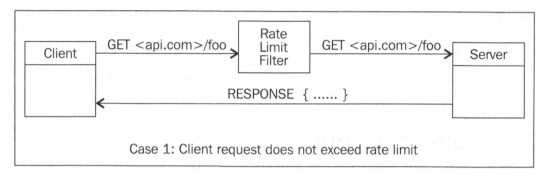

The preceding diagram shows a client making a GET request to `http://api.com/foo`. The **Rate Limit Filter** checks the access count of the client based on the IP address. As the client does not exceed the rate limit, the request is forwarded to the server. The server can return a JSON or XML or a text response.

The following diagram shows the client making a GET request to `http://api.com/foo`. The **Rate Limit Filter** checks the access count of the client based on the IP address. Since the client exceeds the rate limit, the request is not forwarded to the server, and the Rate Limiter returns an error code of `429 Too Many Requests` in the HTTP response.

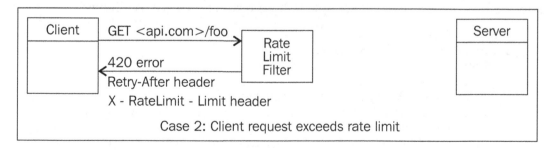

A detailed look at the rate-limiting sample

To implement a rate limiter with JAX-RS, we need to implement a `Filter` class.
This is shown in the following code snippet:

```
@WebFilter(filterName = "RateLimiter",
        urlPatterns = {"/*"}
        )
public class RateLimiter implements Filter {
    private static final int REQ_LIMIT = 3;
    private static final int TIME_LIMIT = 600000;
    private static AccessCounter accessCounter =
      AccessCounter.getInstance();
}
```

The preceding snippet shows an implementation of the `WebFilter` interface of the
`javax.servlet.annotation` package. The `@WebFilter` annotation indicates that
this class is a filter for the application.

The `@WebFilter` annotation must have at least one `urlPatterns` or `value` attribute
in the annotation.

The `REQ_LIMIT` constant stands for the number of requests that can be made in a time
period. The `TIME_LIMIT` constant stands for the time duration for the rate limit after
which new requests from a client can be accepted.

For simplicity, we have smaller limit values in the samples. In real-world scenarios,
the limits could be, for example, 60 requests per minute or 1,000 requests per day.
If the request count reaches the limit, the `Retry-After` header will indicate the time
for which the client will have to wait before the server can process the next request.

To keep track of the request count associated with a client, we have created
a class called `AccessCounter`. Here is the code for the `AccessCounter` class.
The `AccessCounter` class is a `Singleton` class annotated with `@Singleton`.
It stores a `ConcurrentHashMap` class that contains IP addresses as the keys
and data related to the client, known as `AccessData`, as values.

```
@Singleton
public class AccessCounter {

    private static AccessCounter accessCounter;

    private static ConcurrentHashMap<String,AccessData> accessDetails
= new ConcurrentHashMap<String, AccessData>();
}
```

The `AccessData` class is responsible for storing the details for a client, such as the number of requests and when the last request was made. It is a simple **Plain Old Java Object (POJO)**, as shown in the following code snippet:

```
public class AccessData {
    private long lastUpdated;
    private AtomicInteger count;

    public long getLastUpdated() {
        return lastUpdated;
    }

    public void setLastUpdated(long lastUpdated) {
        this.lastUpdated = lastUpdated;
    }

    public AtomicInteger getCount() {
        return count;
    }

    public void setCount(AtomicInteger count) {
        this.count = count;
    }
}

...
```

As shown in the preceding snippet, the `AccessData` class has a field called `count` and a field called `lastUpdated`. Whenever a new request arrives, the count is incremented, and the `lastUpdated` field is set to the current time.

The `doFilter()` method of the `RateLimiter` class is used in the following code snippet:

```
@Override
    public void doFilter(ServletRequest servletRequest,
        ServletResponse servletResponse,
                        FilterChain filterChain) throws
                            IOException, ServletException {

        HttpServletRequest httpServletRequest =
            (HttpServletRequest) servletRequest;
        HttpServletResponse httpServletResponse =
            (HttpServletResponse) servletResponse;

        String ipAddress = getIpAddress(httpServletRequest);
        if (accessCounter.contains(ipAddress)) {
```

```
        if (!requestLimitExceeded(ipAddress)) {
            accessCounter.increment(ipAddress);
            accessCounter.getAccessDetails(ipAddress
               ).setLastUpdated(System.currentTimeMillis());

        } else {

            httpServletResponse.addIntHeader(
               "Retry-After",TIME_LIMIT);
            httpServletResponse.sendError(429);

        }
    } else {
        accessCounter.add(ipAddress);

    }
    filterChain.doFilter(servletRequest, servletResponse)

}
```

The preceding code shows the doFilter() method of the javax.servlet.Filter class, which is overridden in the RateLimiter implementation. In this method, the IP address of the client is first determined.

If the accessCounter class contains the IP address, a check is made to see if the request limit has exceeded in the requestLimitExceeded() method.

If the rate limit has exceeded, then the Retry-After headers are sent in the httpServletResponse along with a 429 Too Many Requests error. If there is a new request that comes from the same client after some time, and it is greater than the TIME_LIMIT value, then the counter is reset back to 0, and the request from the client can be processed again.

The following are the headers for rate limiting that can be sent back in the response to the client:

- X-RateLimit-Limit: The maximum number of requests that the client can make during a specific time period
- X-RateLimit-Remaining: The number of requests remaining in the current rate-limit window

A detailed sample is included with this book. After the sample is deployed on an application server, the client can make multiple requests to get order details for coffees.

For the sake of simplicity, we have enforced the rate limit as 3 and the time limit as 10 minutes. The following is a sample `curl` request:

```
curl -i http://localhost:8080/ratelimiting/v1/coffees/1
HTTP/1.1 200 OK
X-Powered-By: Servlet/3.1 JSP/2.3 (GlassFish Server Open Source Edition
4.0  Java/Oracle Corporation/1.7)
Server: GlassFish Server Open Source Edition  4.0
Content-Type: application/json
Date: Mon, 23 Jun 2014 23:27:34 GMT
Content-Length: 57


{
  "name":"Mocha",
  "order":1,
  "size":"Small",
  "type":"Brewed"
}
```

Once the rate limit has been crossed, you will see a `429` error:

```
curl -i http://localhost:8080/ratelimiting/v1/coffees/1
HTTP/1.1 429 CUSTOM
X-Powered-By: Servlet/3.1 JSP/2.3 (GlassFish Server Open Source Edition
4.0  Java/Oracle Corporation/1.7)
Server: GlassFish Server Open Source Edition  4.0
Retry-After: 600000
Content-Language:
Content-Type: text/html
Date: Mon, 23 Jun 2014 23:29:04 GMT
Content-Length: 1098
```

> This sample showed how to build your custom filters to implement rate limiting. Another option is to use an open source project called **Repose**, which is a scalable and extensive rate-limiting implementation. Repose is an open source HTTP proxy service that provides rate-limiting, client-authentication, versioning, and so on. For more details, check http://openrepose.org/.

In the next section, we will discuss the best practices that must be followed to avoid reaching rate limits when consuming a REST API.

Best practices to avoid reaching the rate limits

Here are the best practices that can be followed to avoid reaching rate limits when consuming a REST API.

Caching

Caching API responses on the server side can help avoid reaching the rate limits. Setting reasonable expiry time intervals ensures the database is not thrashed with queries, and responses can be sent from the cache if the resource has not changed. For example, an application that displays tweets fetched from Twitter can cache the response from the Twitter API or use the Twitter Streaming API (covered in the following section). Ideally, API consumers should not make identical requests more than once a minute. This is generally a waste of bandwidth, as in most cases the exact same result will be returned.

Not making calls in loops

It is a good practice to not make API requests inside loops. The server API should be designed to be as verbose as possible and help the clients by sending as much detail as possible in the response. This ensures the consumers can fetch a collection of objects in one API operation instead of fetching individual objects inside a loop.

Logging requests

It is a good practice to use logging on the client side to see how many requests the client is making. Observing the logs will help the clients analyze as to which are the non-redundant queries that add to the rate limits and can be eliminated.

Avoiding polling

Additionally, consumers should not poll for changes. Instead of polling to see if the content has changed, the client can use WebHooks (`http://en.wikipedia.org/wiki/Webhook`) or Push Notifications (`http://en.wikipedia.org/wiki/Push_technology`) to receive a notification. More details on WebHooks will be given in *Chapter 6, Emerging Standards and the Future of REST*.

Supporting the streaming API

API developers can support a streaming API. This can help the client avoid reaching the rate limits. The set of streaming APIs offered by Twitter gives developers low latency access to Twitter's global stream of tweet data. A streaming client does not need to bear the overhead, associated with polling a REST endpoint and will get messages indicating tweets and other events that have occurred.

Once applications establish a connection to a streaming endpoint, they are delivered a feed of tweets, without worrying about polling or REST API rate limits.

Case study of Twitter REST API rate limits

Twitter has a rate limit of 150 requests per hour per unauthenticated client.

OAuth calls are permitted 350 requests per hour based on the access token in the request.

An application that exceeds the rate limitations of the Search API will receive an HTTP 420 response code. The best practice is to watch for this error condition and honor the Retry-After header that is returned. The Retry-After header's value is the number of seconds the client application should wait before requesting data from the Search API again. In case the client sends more than the allowed requests per hour, the client gets a 420 Enhance Your Calm error.

420 Enhance Your Calm (Twitter)

This is not part of the HTTP standard but returned by the Twitter Search and Trends API when the client is being rate-limited. Applications should ideally implement the 429 Too Many Requests response code instead.

Response pagination

REST APIs are consumed by other systems from web to mobile clients and hence, responses that return multiple items should be paged with a certain number of items per page. This is known as Response pagination. Along with the response, it is always good to add some additional metadata about the total count of objects, the total number of pages, and the links that refer to the next set of results. The consumers can specify a page index to query for results and the number of results per page.

Implementing and documenting default settings for the number of results per page is a recommended practice in case the client does not specify the number of results per page. For example, GitHub's REST API sets the default page size to 30 records with a maximum of 100, and sets a rate limit on the number of times the client can query the API. If the API has a default page size, then the query string can just specify the page index.

The following section covers the different types of pagination techniques that can be used. API developers may choose to implement one or more of these techniques based on their use cases.

Types of pagination

The following are the different techniques of pagination that can be used:

- Offset-based pagination
- Time-based pagination
- Cursor-based pagination

Offset-based pagination

Offset-based pagination is the case when the client wants results specified by a page number and the number of results per page. For example, if a client wants to query all the details of books checked out, or the coffees ordered, they can send in a query request as follows:

```
GET v1/coffees/orders?page=1&limit=50
```

The following table details what query parameters the offset-based pagination would include:

Query parameter	Description
page	This specifies which page to return
limit	This specifies the number of maximum results per page that can be included in the response

Time-based pagination

The time-based pagination technique will be used when the client wants to query for a set of results between a specific timeframe.

For example, to get a list of coffees ordered between a specific timeframe, a client can send in a query as follows:

```
GET v1/coffees/orders?since=140358321&until=143087472
```

The following table details what query parameters a time-based pagination would include:

Query parameter	Description
until:	This is a Unix timestamp that points to the end of the time range
since	This is a Unix timestamp that points to the beginning of the time range
limit	This specifies the number of max results per page that can be included in the response

Cursor-based pagination

The cursor-based pagination is a technique where the results are separated into pages by a cursor, and the results can be navigated forwards and backwards using the next and previous cursors that are provided in the response.

The cursor-based pagination API avoids returning duplicate records in cases where additional resources are added between pagination requests. This is because the cursor parameter is a pointer that indicates where to resume the results from, for the subsequent call.

Twitter and cursor-based pagination

Here is an example of how Twitter uses cursor-based pagination. A query to get the IDs of a user who has a large number of followers could be paginated and returned in the following format:

```
{
    "ids": [
        385752029,
        602890434,
        ...
        333181469,
        333165023
    ],
    "next_cursor": 1374004777531007833,
    "next_cursor_str": "1374004777531007833",
    "previous_cursor": 0,
    "previous_cursor_str": "0"
}
```

The `next_cursor` value could be passed to the next query to get the next set of results:

```
GET https://api.twitter.com/1.1/followers/ids.json?
screen_name=someone &cursor=1374004777531007833
```

Using the `next_cursor` and the `previous_cursor` values, it is easy to navigate between the set of results.

Now that we have covered the different pagination techniques, let's go over a sample in detail. The following sample shows how to implement a simple offset-based pagination technique with JAX-RS.

The project's layout

The project's directory layout follows the standard Maven structure, which is briefly explained in the following table.

The example used is that of a coffee shop service that can be queried for all orders placed so far.

Source code	Description
src/main/java	This directory contains all the sources required by the coffee shop application

Here is the `CoffeeResource` class:

```
@Path("v1/coffees")
public class CoffeesResource {
    @GET
    @Path("orders")
    @Produces(MediaType.APPLICATION_JSON)
    public List<Coffee> getCoffeeList(
@QueryParam("page")  @DefaultValue("1") int page,
                                @QueryParam("limit") @
DefaultValue("10") int limit ) {
        return CoffeeService.getCoffeeList( page, limit);

    }
}
```

The `getCoffeeList()` method takes two `QueryParam` values: `page` and `limit`. The `page` QueryParam value corresponds to the page index and `limit` corresponds to the number of results per page. The `@DefaultValue` annotation specifies the default values that can be used if the query parameters are absent.

Here is the output when the sample is run. The `metadata` element contains details of the `totalCount` value that is the total number of records. Additionally, there is the `links` attribute of `JSONArray` that contains details such as `self`, which is the current page, and `next`, which is the next link to fetch more results.

```
{
    "metadata": {
        "resultsPerPage": 10,
        "totalCount": 100,
        "links": [
            {
                "self": "/orders?page=1&limit=10"
            },
```

```
            {
                "next": "/orders?page=2&limit=10"
            }
        ]
    },
    "coffees": [
        {
            "Id": 10,
            "Name": "Expresso",
            "Price": 2.77,
            "Type": "Hot",
            "Size": "Large"
        },
        {
            "Id": 11,
            "Name": "Cappuchino",
            "Price": 0.14,
            "Type": "Brewed",
            "Size": "Large"
        },
    .....
        ......
    ]
}
```

The sample is bundled with this book's downloadable source code bundle.

 It is always a good practice to include the default values for the number of results per page in REST API for pagination. Also, it is recommended that the API developers add metadata on the response, so consumers of the API can fetch additional information easily to get the next set of results.

Internationalization and localization

Often, services need to operate in a global environment and responses need to be tailored based on the country and locale. Localization parameters can be specified in one of the following fields:

- HTTP headers
- Query parameters
- Content of the REST response

Language negotiation is similar to content negotiation; the HTTP header `Accept-Language` can take different language codes based on any two-letter initial for ISO-3166 country codes (`http://www.iso.org/iso/country_codes.htm`). The `Content-Language` header is similar to the `Content-Type` header and can specify the language for the response.

For example, here is a `Content-Language` header sent in the response to a request sent by a client:

```
HTTP/1.1 200 OK
X-Powered-By: Servlet/3.1 JSP/2.3 (GlassFish Server Open Source
   Edition  4.0  Java/Oracle Corporation/1.7)
Server: GlassFish Server Open Source Edition  4.0
Content-Language: en
Content-Type: text/html
Date: Mon, 23 Jun 2014 23:29:04 GMT
Content-Length: 1098
```

The preceding response sets `Content-Language` to en as part of the response.

JAX-RS supports runtime content negotiation using the `javax.ws.rs.core.Variant` class and `Request` objects. The `Variant` class may contain a media type, a language, and an encoding. The `Variant.VariantListBuilder` class is used to build a list of representation variants.

The following code snippet shows how to create a list of resource representation variants:

```
List<Variant> variantList =
    Variant.
       .languages("en", "fr").build();
```

The preceding code snippet calls the build method of the `VariantListBuilder` class with languages `"en"` and `"fr"`.

Query parameters can include locale-specific information so that the server can return the information in that language.

The following is an example:

```
GET v1/books?locale=fr
```

This query shows an example that will include the locale in the query parameter to get details of books. Additionally, the content of the REST response can contain country-specific details such as currency codes, and other details based on the HTTP headers or the query parameters sent in the request.

Miscellaneous topics

The following sections cover some details on miscellaneous topics such as HATEOAS, and Extensibility in REST.

HATEOAS

Hypermedia as the Engine of Application State (HATEOAS) is a constraint of the REST application architecture.

A hypermedia-driven API gives details about the APIs that are available and the corresponding actions that can be taken by the consumer, by providing hypermedia links in the response sent by the server.

For example, a book representation for a REST resource that contains data such as the name and ISBN would look as follows:

```
{
    "Name":" Developing RESTful Services with JAX-RS 2.0,
            WebSockets, and JSON",
    "ISBN": "1782178120"
}
```

A HATEOAS implementation would return the following:

```
{
    "Name":" Developing RESTful Services with JAX-RS 2.0,
            WebSockets, and JSON",
    "ISBN": "1782178120"
    "links": [
       {
        "rel": "self",
        "href": "http://packt.com/books/123456789"
       }
    ]
}
```

In the preceding sample, the `links` element has the `rel` and `href` JSON objects.

The `rel` attribute in this example is a self-referencing hyperlink. More complex systems might include other relationships. For example, a book order might have a `"rel":"customer"` relationship, linking the book order to its customer. `href` is a complete URL that uniquely defines the resource.

The advantage of HATEOAS is that it helps client developers explore the protocol. The links give client developers a hint as to what may be the possible next action to take. While there is no standard for hypermedia controls, the recommendations are to follow the ATOM RFC (4287).

> According to the Richardson Maturity Model, HATEOAS is considered the final level of REST. This means that each link is presumed to implement the standard REST verbs of GET, POST, PUT, and DELETE. Adding details using the links element as shown in the preceding code snippet gives the client the information they need to navigate the service and take the next action.

The PayPal REST API and HATEOAS

PayPal REST API provides HATEOAS support, so with every response, there is a collection of links that can help the consumer decide the next action to take.

For example, a sample response from the PayPal REST API includes the JSON objects shown in the following code:

```
{
    "href": "https://www.sandbox.paypal.com/webscr?cmd
       =_express-checkout&token=EC-60U79048BN7719609",
    "rel": "approval_url",
    "method": "REDIRECT"
},
{
    "href": "https://api.sandbox.paypal.com/v1/payments/
       payment/PAY-6RV70583SB702805EKEYSZ6Y/execute",
    "rel": "execute",
    "method": "POST"
}
```

A brief description of the attributes is as follows.

- href: This contains information about URLs that can be used for future REST API calls
- rel: This link shows how it is related to the previous REST API calls
- method: This shows which method is to be used for the REST API calls

> For more details, check https://developer.paypal.com/docs/integration/direct/paypal-rest-payment-hateoas-links/.

REST and extensibility

RESTful applications are more extensible as well as more maintainable over time. RESTful applications based on constraints of the design style are easier to understand and work with, mainly due to their simplicity. They are also more predictable, since it's all about the resources. Also, RESTful applications are easier to work with as opposed to an XML-RPC application, where the consumer needs to parse a complex WSDL document to even begin to understand what's happening.

Additional topics for the REST API

The following section lists additional topics that may be useful for REST developers. We have covered topics in earlier chapters, from the designing of RESTful services, error handling, validations, authentication, and caching to rate limiting. This section focuses on additional utilities to empower the REST API developer with better testing and documentation.

Testing RESTful services

It is always efficient to have an automated set of tests, which can validate responses sent by the server. One such framework to build automated tests for RESTful services is REST Assured.

REST Assured is the Java DSL for easy testing of RESTful services. It supports GET, PUT, POST, HEAD, OPTIONS, and PATCH, and can be used to validate as well as verify responses that the server sends.

The following is an example of getting a coffee order and verifying the ID returned in the response:

```
get("order").
then().assertThat().
body("coffee.id",equalTo(5));
```

In the preceding snippet, we make a call to get a coffee order and verify that the coffee.id value is 5.

REST Assured supports specifying and validating, for example, parameters, headers, cookies, and body easily. It also supports mapping Java objects to and from JSON and XML. For more details, you can check https://code.google. com/p/rest-assured/.

Documenting RESTful services

It is always a good practice to provide documentation on the RESTful services built for the consumers, whether they are from within the same enterprise or whether the consumer is an external application or a mobile client. The following section covers some frameworks for providing good documentation for RESTful services.

Swagger is a framework implementation for describing, producing, consuming, and visualizing RESTful web services. The documentation of methods, parameters, and models are tightly integrated into the server code. Swagger is language-agnostic and implementations for Scala, Java, and HTML5 are available.

The tutorial on how to add Swagger to the REST API is found at the following URL:

```
https://github.com/wordnik/swagger-core/wiki/Adding-Swagger-to-your-
API
```

Recommended reading

The following links refer to some of the topics that are covered in this chapter, and they will be useful to review and get detailed information:

- `https://dev.twitter.com/docs`: The Twitter API documentation
- `https://dev.twitter.com/console`: The Twitter Developer console
- `https://dev.twitter.com/docs/rate-limiting/1.1`: The Twitter API rate limiting in v1.1
- `https://dev.twitter.com/docs/misc/cursoring`: The Twitter API and cursoring
- `https://dev.twitter.com/docs/api/streaming`: The Twitter streaming APIs
- `https://developers.facebook.com/docs/reference/ads-api/api-rate-limiting/`: Facebook API rate limiting
- `https://developer.github.com/v3/rate_limit/`: GitHub API rate limiting
- `https://developers.facebook.com/docs/opengraph/guides/internationalization/`: Facebook localization

Summary

This chapter covered advanced topics that every RESTful API developer should know. In the beginning, we saw the rate-limiting sample that demonstrated how to enforce throttling so that the server is not blasted with API calls. We also saw how Twitter, GitHub, and Facebook APIs enforce rate limiting. We covered different pagination techniques and a basic pagination sample and best practices. Then, we moved on to internationalization and other miscellaneous topics. Finally, we covered HATEOAS and how it is the next level of REST API, REST, and extensibility topics.

The next chapter will cover other emerging standards such as WebSockets, WebHooks, and the role of REST in the future of evolving web standards.

6
Emerging Standards and the Future of REST

This chapter covers the emerging and evolving technologies that will augment the functionality of RESTful services and provide some perspective on the future of REST as well as other real-time API supporters. We will cover some of the real-time APIs and see how they can help with respect to older ways such as polling. Given the ubiquitous popularity of platforms such as Twitter, Facebook, and Stripe, it is no surprise that they have adopted a paradigm shift and thus provide real-time APIs to give information to the client as and when an event occurs.

This chapter will cover the following topics:

- Real-time APIs
- Polling
- WebHooks
- WebSockets
- Additional real-time API supporters, which include the following:
    - PubSubHubbub
    - Server-sent events
    - XMPP
    - BOSH over XMPP

- Case studies on companies using WebHooks and WebSockets
- Comparison between WebHooks and WebSockets
- REST and Micro Services

We will start with defining what a real-time API refers to, and then, we will cover polling and its disadvantages. Next, we will walk through the different models that are widely used for asynchronous real-time communication. Finally, we will elaborate the pragmatic approaches to WebHooks and WebSockets in detail.

Real-time APIs

In our context, a real-time API helps the API consumer receive the events that they are interested in, as they occur. An example of a real-time update is when someone posts a link on Facebook or someone you follow on Twitter tweets about a topic. Another example of a real-time API is to receive the feed of stock price changes as they occur.

Polling

Polling is the most traditional way to get data from a data source that produces the stream of events and updates. The client makes requests periodically, and the server sends data if there is a response. In case there is no data to be sent by the server, an empty response is returned. The following diagram shows how continuous polling works:

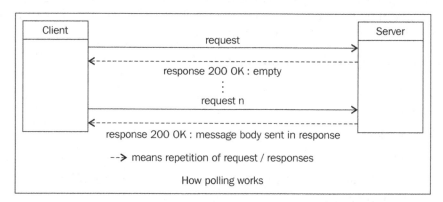

How polling works

Polling comes with multiple drawbacks such as empty responses for requests made when there is no update on the server; this results in waste of bandwidth and processing time. Polling with lower frequencies will result in the client missing the updates close to the time the updates happen, and polling too frequently results in waste of resources as well as facing the rate limitation imposed by the server.

To eliminate these drawbacks of polling, we will cover the following topics:

- The PuSH model — PubSubHubbub
- The streaming model

The PuSH model – PubSubHubbub

PuSH is a simple topic based on the publish/subscribe protocol, which is based on ATOM/RSS. Its goal is to convert atom feeds to real-time data and eliminate the polling that affects the consumers of the feeds. The subscribers register their interests in a topic, and the original publisher tells the interested subscribers that there is something new that interests them.

To distribute the tasks of publishing and content distributing, there is a notion of the **Hub**, which can be delegated to send the content to the subscribers. The following diagram depicts the PubSubHubbub model:

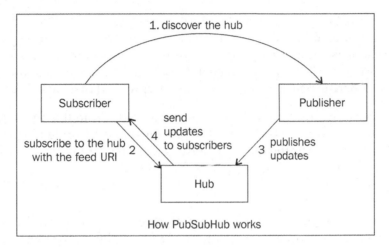

How PubSubHub works

Let's look at how this model works:

1. The **Subscriber** discovers the **Hub** by fetching the feed from the **Publisher**.
2. Once the **Hub** is discovered, the **Subscriber** subscribes to the **Hub** with the feed URI it is interested in.
3. Now, when the **Publisher** has updates to send, it will let the **Hub** get the updates.
4. The **Hub** then sends the updates to all the publishers.

The advantage of this model is that the publisher does not have to be concerned with sending updates to all the subscribers. Also, on the other end, the subscribers have an advantage as they get the updates from the hub as and when they occur, without continuously polling the publisher.

The **WebHooks** paradigm, discussed in the subsequent sections, uses this protocol.

The streaming model

The streaming model for asynchronous communication involves keeping a channel open and sending the data as it occurs. In this case, a socket connection needs to be kept open.

Server-sent events

Server-sent events (SSE) is a technology based on the streaming model, where a browser gets automatic updates from a server via an HTTP connection. The W3C has standardized the Server-Sent Events EventSource API as part of HTML5.

With SSEs, the client initiates a request to the server using the `"text/eventstream"` MimeType. Once the initial handshake has taken place, the server can keep sending events to the client as and when they occur. The events are plain text messages sent from the server to the clients. They can be data that can be consumed in the client side by the event listener, and the event listener can interpret and react to the received event.

SSEs define a message format for the events that are sent from the server to the clients. The message format is composed of plain text line separated by a stream of characters. Lines that carry the message body or data start with `data:` and end with `\n\n`, as shown in the following snippet:

```
data: My message \n\n
```

Lines that carry some **Quality of Service (QoS)** directives (for example, `retry` and `id`) start with the QoS attribute name, followed by `:`, and then the QoS attribute's value. The standard format makes it possible to develop generic libraries around SSE to make software development easier.

The following diagram shows how SSEs work:

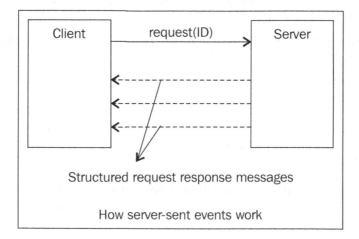

How server-sent events work

As shown in the diagram, the client subscribes to an event source. The server keeps sending updates as and when they occur.

Additionally, the server can associate and send IDs along with the whole message, as shown in the following code snippet:

```
id: 12345\n
data: Message1\n
data: Message 2\n\n
```

The preceding snippet shows how multiline messages with event IDs and data can be sent, with the last line that terminates with two \n\n characters.

Setting an ID lets the client keep track of the last event fired so that if the connection to the server is dropped, a special HTTP header (Last-Event-ID) is set with the new request sent by the client.

The upcoming sections cover how to associate IDs with SSEs, how SSE works with connection loss and retries, and how to associate event names with SSEs.

Associating an ID with an event

Each SSE message can have a message identifier, which can be used for a variety of purposes, for example, to keep track of the messages that the client has received and also to keep a checkpoint for it. When the message ID is used in SSE, the client can supply the last message ID as one of the connection parameters to instruct the server to resume from a specific message onwards. Of course, the server-side code should implement a proper procedure to resume a communication from the message ID as requested by the client.

An example of the SSE message with the ID is shown in the following snippet:

```
id: 123 \n
data: This is a single line event \n\n
```

Retrying in case of connection failures

Firefox, Chrome, Opera, and Safari support server-sent events. In case there is a connection loss between the browser and server, the browser can try reconnecting to the server. There is a retry directive, which can be configured by the server to enable the retries from a client. The default value for the retry interval is 3 seconds. To increase the retry interval to 5 seconds, the server can send a retry event as shown:

```
retry: 5000\n
data: This is a single line data\n\n
```

Associating event names with events

Another SSE directive is the event name. Each event source can generate more than one type of event, and a client can decide how to consume each event type based on what event type it subscribes for. The following code snippet shows how the `name` event directive incorporates into the message:

```
event: bookavailable\n
data: {"name" : "Game of Thrones"}\n\n
event: newbookadded\n
data: {"name" :"Storm of Swords"}\n\n
```

Server-sent events and JavaScript

The API that is considered the foundation of SSE in the client side for JavaScript developers is the `EventSource` interface. The `EventSource` interface contains a fair number of functions and attributes, but the most important ones are listed in the following table:

Function name	Description
addEventListener	This function adds an event listener to handle the incoming events based on the event type.
removeEventListener	This function removes an already registered listener.
onmessage	This function is invoked on message arrival. There is no custom event handling available when using the `onmessage` method. Listeners manage the custom event handling.
onerror	This function is invoked when something goes wrong with the connection.
onopen	This function is invoked when a connection is opened.
onclose	This function is invoked when a connection is closed.

The following snippet shows how to subscribe for different event types omitted by one source. The snippet assumes that the incoming messages are JSON-formatted messages. For example, there is an application that can stream updates to users as and when new books are available in some storage. The `'bookavailable'` listener uses a simple JSON parser to parse the incoming JSON.

Then, it will use this to update the GUI, while the `'newbookadded'` listener uses the reviver function to filter out and selectively process the JSON pairs.

```
var source = new EventSource('books');
source.addEventListener('bookavailable', function(e) {
  var data = JSON.parse(e.data);
  // use data to update some GUI element...
}, false);

source.addEventListener('newbookadded', function(e) {
  var data = JSON.parse(e.data, function (key, value) {
    var type;
    if (value && typeof value === 'string') {
return "String value is: "+value;
    }
    return value;
```

Server-sent events and Jersey

SSEs are not part of the standard JAX-RS specification. However, they are supported in the Jersey implementation of JAX-RS. For more details, check out `https://jersey.java.net/documentation/latest/sse.html`.

WebHooks

WebHooks are a form of user-defined custom HTTP callbacks. With the WebHook model, a client provides the event producer with an endpoint to which the event producer can *post* the events. When an event is posted to the endpoint, the client application that is interested in such events can take appropriate actions. An example of WebHooks is triggering an event such as a Hudson job using a GIT post-receive hook.

To acknowledge that the subscriber received the WebHook without any problem, the subscriber's endpoint should return a `200 OK HTTP` status code. The event producer will ignore the request body and any other request header, other than the status. Any response code outside the 200 ranges, including 3xx codes, will indicate that they did not receive the WebHook, and the API might retry sending the HTTP `POST` request.

WebHooks events generated by GitHub deliver a payload of information about activity in a repository. WebHooks can trigger across several different actions. For example, a consumer might request for a payload of information any time a commit is made, a repository is forked, or an issue is created.

The following diagram depicts how WebHooks work with GitHub or GitLab:

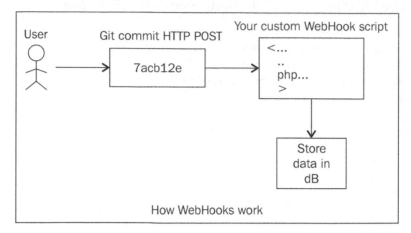

How WebHooks work

Let's look at how WebHooks work:

1. The user makes a **Git** push.

2. There is a custom WebHook URL to post the event object registered by the consumer with GitHub. When an event occurs, for example, when a commit is made, the GitHub service will send the payload of information regarding the commit, using a **POST** message to the endpoint provided by the consumer.

3. The consumer application can then store data in the **dB** or take some other action such as triggering a continuous integration build.

> **Some of the popular WebHooks case studies**
>
> Twilio uses WebHooks to send SMS messages. GitHub uses WebHooks to send repository change notification and, optionally, some payloads.
>
> PayPal uses **Instant Payment Notification (IPN)**, a message service that automatically notifies merchants of events related to PayPal transactions, and it is based on WebHooks.
>
> Facebook's real-time API uses WebHooks and is based on **PubSubHubbub (PuSH)**.

As mentioned earlier, if an API does not offer a form of WebHooks for notification, its consumers will have to keep polling for data, which is not only inefficient but also not real time.

WebSockets

The WebSocket protocol is a protocol that provides full-duplex communication channels over a single TCP connection.

The WebSocket protocol is an independent TCP-based protocol, and its only relationship to HTTP is that the handshake to switch over to WebSockets is interpreted by HTTP servers as an Upgrade request.

It provides the option to have full-duplex, real-time communication between clients (for example, a web browser) and an endpoint without the constant cost of establishing a connection or polling resource intensively. WebSockets are extensively used in social feeds, multiplayer games, collaborative editing, and so on.

The following lines show a WebSocket Protocol handshake, which starts with an Upgrade request:

```
GET /text HTTP/1.1\r\n Upgrade: WebSocket\r\n Connection:
   Upgrade\r\n Host: www.websocket.org\r\n …\r\n
HTTP/1.1 101 WebSocket Protocol Handshake\r\n
Upgrade: WebSocket\r\n
Connection: Upgrade\r\n
…\r\n
```

The following diagram shows an example of a handshake with the HTTP/1.1 Upgrade request and HTPP/1.1 Switching Protocols response:

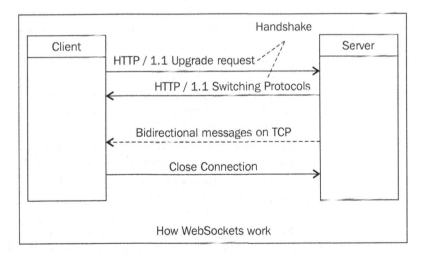

How WebSockets work

Once the connection has been established between the client and the server with the Upgrade request and HTTP/1.1 response, WebSocket data frames, binary or text, can be sent back and forth between the client and server from both directions.

WebSockets data is minimally framed between 2 bytes; this dramatically reduces the overhead compared to what HTTP headers would transfer.

A very basic example of using the JavaScript WebSockets API is shown as follows:

```
//Constructionof the WebSocket object
var websocket = new WebSocket("coffee");
//Setting the message event Function
websocket.onmessage = function(evt) {
onMessageFunc(evt)
};
//onMessageFunc which when a message arrives is invoked.
function onMessageFunc (evt) {
//Perform some GUI update depending the message content
}
//Sending a message to the server
websocket.send("coffee.selected.id=1020");
//Setting an event listener for the event type "open".
addEventListener('open', function(e){
        onOpenFunc(evt)});

//Close the connection.
websocket.close();
```

The following table will describe the WebSockets functionality and various functions in detail:

Function name	Description
send	This function can be used to send a message to the server's specified URL.
onopen	This function is invoked when the connection is created. The onopen function handles the open event type.
onmessage	When a new message arrives, the onmessage function is invoked to handle the message event.
onclose	This function is invoked when the connection is being closed. The onclose method handles the close event type.
onerror	This function is invoked to handle the error event when an error occurs in the communication channel.
close	This function is used to close the communication socket and end the interaction between the client and server.

Popular WebSockets Case Studies

Zynga Poker is one of the first games to utilize WebSockets connections on a massive scale. Using WebSockets in Zynga Poker HTML5 delivers a smooth, high-speed gameplay that allows for a synchronous experience on the mobile web. It varies based on connections, but the game loads and refreshes almost immediately.

Additional real-time API supporters

There are some more commonly used real-time or near real-time communication protocols and APIs that are mostly used outside of the browser. Some of these protocols and APIs are described in the subsequent sections.

XMPP

The XMPP protocol was developed to address the requirements of text messaging and Internet-chat-oriented solutions. XMPP's basic model of communication is client to server, server to server, server to client. In support of this, it defines a client to server protocol and a server to server protocol based on XML messages encoded and transmitted directly over TCP.

XMPP is a mature protocol with many implementations in different languages and platforms. The main drawback associated with XMPP is the long polling and open sockets to handle the inbound and outbound communications.

BOSH over XMPP

Bidirectional streams Over Synchronous HTTP (BOSH) specified in XEP-0124 is the standardized way to do XMPP over HTTP. For the client-initiated protocol, the client simply sends XMPP packets on HTTP, and for the server-initiated protocol, the server uses long polling with the connection open for a prespecified period of time.

The main advantage of BOSH is the possibility that it provides to use a web browser as an XMPP client by taking advantage of any of the JavaScript implementations of BOSH. Emite, JSJaC, and xmpp4js are some of the libraries that support BOSH.

Comparisons between WebHooks, WebSockets, and server-sent events

SSEs are sent over HTTP unlike WebSockets. SSEs offer only one-way communication of events from the server to the client and do not support a full-duplex communication as WebSockets do. SSEs have the ability to automatically retry a connection; they also have event IDs that can be associated with messages to provide **Quality of Service (QoS)** features. The WebSockets specification does not support these features.

On the other hand, WebSockets support full-duplex communication, and reduce the latency and help improve throughput, as there is an initial handshake over HTTP, but then, the messages are transferred between endpoints over TCP.

In comparison to the two protocols mentioned earlier, WebHooks has a lower barrier to entry and offers an easy way for applications and services to integrate with one another. This enables the capability of having an interconnected and interchangeable set of loosely coupled cloud services talking to each other via HTTP requests.

The following table compares and contrasts WebHooks, WebSockets, and SSEs in different areas:

Criteria	WebHooks	WebSockets	Server-sent events
Asynchronous real-time communication support	Yes	Yes	Yes
Callback URL registered	Yes	No	No
Long-lived open connection	No	Yes	Yes
Bidirectional	No	Yes	No
Error handling	No	Yes	Yes
Easy to support and implement	Yes	Needs browsers and proxy server support	Yes
Needs fallback to polling	No	Yes	No

The next section will cover how highly available cloud applications are moving toward the Micro Services-based architecture.

REST and Micro Services

The dream of SOA has become a reality with the emergence of Micro Services architecture, which comprises breaking a monolithic application into sets of fine-grained services. We will now look at the different advantages of Micro Services as compared to monolithic services.

Simplicity

Instead of using the more complicated traditional enterprise, many developers are finding that building the same application using lightweight API services proves to be more resilient, scalable, and maintainable. This style is the Micro Services-based architecture. This is in contrast with approaches such as the legacy RPC approaches of CORBA and RMI, or the bulky Web Services protocols such as SOAP.

Isolation of problems

In the monolithic applications, all the components of a service are loaded in a single application artifact (a WAR, EAR, or JAR file), which is deployed on a single JVM. This implies that if the application or the application server goes down, it would mean a failure of all the services.

However, with the Micro Services architecture, the services can be independent WAR/EAR files. The services can communicate with one another with REST and JSON, or XML. Another way to communicate between services in the Micro Services architecture is to use a messaging protocol such as AMQP/Rabbit MQ.

Scale up and scale down

With monolithic services, not all services in the deployed application's file might need to be scaled, but they all are forced to follow the same scale-up and scale-down rules laid down at deployment level.

With the Micro Services architecture, applications can be built by smaller services that can be deployed and scaled independently. This results in an architecture that is resilient to failures, scalable and agile, for developing, building, and deploying services quickly from the feature definition phase to production phase.

Clear separation of capabilities

In the Micro Services architecture, these services can be organized based on business capabilities. For example, an inventory service can be separated from a billing service, which can be separate from a shipping service. In case one of the services fails, the others can still continue serving requests as mentioned in the *Isolation of Problems* section.

Language independence

Another advantage of the Micro Services architecture is that the services are built with a simple and easy-to-consume REST/JSON-based API that can be easily consumed by other languages or frameworks such as PHP, Ruby-On-Rails, Python, and node.js.

Amazon and Netflix are some of the pioneers in the Micro Services architecture. eBay has open sourced Turmeric, a comprehensive, policy-driven SOA platform that can be used to develop, deploy, secure, run, and monitor SOA services and consumers.

Recommended reading

The following are the links to additional resources that interested readers can take a look at to get a more complete picture of use cases mentioned in this chapter:

- `https://stripe.com/docs/webhooks`: WebHooks support
- `https://github.com/sockjs`: GitHub SockJs
- `https://developer.github.com/webhooks/testing/`: GitHub WebHooks
- `http://www.twilio.com/platform/webhooks`: Twilio WebHooks
- `http://xmpp4js.sourceforge.net/`: XMPP4JS BOSH library
- `https://code.google.com/p/emite/`: Emite BOSH library

Summary

In this chapter we covered advanced topics such as WebHooks, SSEs, WebSockets, and where and how they are being used in this chapter. One of the primary takeaways from this chapter was to understand how important it is to provide real-time APIs to avoid inefficiencies related to repeated polling. We saw case studies of companies using both WebHooks and WebSockets in their solutions. We saw different best practices and design principles sprinkled throughout the various chapters in the book; this chapter, as a finale, provided a substantial introduction to the future of REST and asynchronous communication. The proliferation of social data has the potential to be a great catalyst for the development of a semantic web that will enable agents to make nontrivial actions on our behalf and get real-time updates using the various patterns we discussed.

Also, we saw how highly available cloud applications tend to move to a networked component model where applications are decomposed into *micro* services, which can be deployed and scaled independently using the Micro Services architecture. For more detailed information on building RESTful services, check out the book *Developing RESTful Services with JAX-RS2.0, WebSockets, and JSON, Bhakti Mehta and Masoud Kalali, Packt Publishing.*

Appendix

In this era of social networking, cloud computing, and mobile applications, people want to be connected to each other, voice opinions, build applications collaboratively, share inputs, and ask questions. This is evident from the data mentioned in `http://www.statisticbrain.com/twitter-statistics/` that shows Twitter has around 6.5 million users and 58 million tweets per day. Similarly, the statistics for Facebook are mindboggling: 1.3 billion users making it the heart of the social web platform. Over the years, GitHub has evolved as the default social coding platform. Thus, Twitter, Facebook, and GitHub are among the most widely used platforms to build applications, mine data, as well as build analytics-related information.

While the previous chapters covered topics such as building RESTful services, adding performance, caching, security, and scaling of RESTful services, this chapter will focus on some popular REST platforms and how they tie in to the different patterns covered in earlier chapters as part of their API infrastructure.

This chapter will cover the following topics:

- Overview of the REST API from GitHub
- Overview of the Open Graph API from Facebook
- Overview of the REST API from Twitter

Overview of the REST API from GitHub

GitHub has become extremely popular as the social collaborative coding platform for building code as well as contributing to other repositories. It is used by developers to create, build, and deploy software, with usage varying from individual projects to various enterprises using it as part of their processes. GitHub has extensive API documentation for its services at `https://developer.github.com/v3/`.

The following section covers in detail how GitHub handles all the different patterns we covered in earlier chapters.

Getting details from GitHub

The following commands show how to use unauthenticated cURL commands to get data for a user, to get details for the repositories, and so on.

The following command gets details for the `javaee-samples` user:

```
curl https://api.github.com/users/javaee-samples
{
  "login": "javaee-samples",
  "id": 6052086,
  "avatar_url": "https://avatars.githubusercontent.com/u/6052086?",
  "gravatar_id": null,
  "url": "https://api.github.com/users/javaee-samples",
  "html_url": "https://github.com/javaee-samples",
  "followers_url": "https://api.github.com/users/javaee-samples/
followers",
  "following_url": "https://api.github.com/users/javaee-samples/
following{/other_user}",
  "gists_url": "https://api.github.com/users/javaee-samples/gists{/gist_
id}",
  "starred_url": "https://api.github.com/users/javaee-samples/starred{/
owner}{/repo}",
  "subscriptions_url": "https://api.github.com/users/javaee-samples/
subscriptions",
  "organizations_url": "https://api.github.com/users/javaee-samples/
orgs",
  "repos_url": "https://api.github.com/users/javaee-samples/repos",
  "events_url": "https://api.github.com/users/javaee-samples/events{/
privacy}",
  "received_events_url": "https://api.github.com/users/javaee-samples/
received_events",
  "type": "Organization",
  "site_admin": false,
  "name": "JavaEE Samples",
  "company": null,
  "blog": "https://arungupta.ci.cloudbees.com/",
  "location": null,
  "email": null,
```

```
"hireable": false,
"bio": null,
"public_repos": 11,
"public_gists": 0,
"followers": 0,
"following": 0,
"created_at": "2013-11-27T17:17:00Z",
"updated_at": "2014-07-03T16:17:51Z"
```

 As shown in the preceding commands, there are different URLs in the preceding response, which can be used to get details such as followers, commits, and so on. This style of presenting the URLs is different from the HATEOAS samples we covered earlier in the book using links, href, rel, and so on. This shows how different platforms choose various ways to provide a connected service, which is self-explanatory.

To get repos for a user with pagination, we can use the query as shown:

```
curl https://api.github.com/users/javaee-samples/repos?page=1&per_page=10
.....
```

GitHub API uses OAuth2 for authenticating users for the requests. All developers working with GitHub API need to register their application. A registered application is assigned a unique client ID and client secret.

For more details on getting authenticated requests for a user, check https://developer.github.com/v3/oauth/.

Verbs and resource actions

The following table covers how GitHub API uses verbs for a specific action to a resource:

Verb	Description
HEAD	This is used to get the HTTP header info
GET	This is used to retrieve resources such as user details
POST	This is used for creating resources such as merging pull requests
PATCH	This is used for partial updates to resources

Verb	Description
PUT	This is used for replacing resources such as updating users
DELETE	This is used for deleting resources such as removing a user as a collaborator

Versioning

GitHub API uses version v3 in its URI. The default version of the API may change in the future. In case the client is depending on a particular version, they recommend sending an Accept header explicitly, as shown:

```
Accept: application/vnd.github.v3+json
```

Error handling

As covered in *Chapter 2*, *Resource Design*, client-side errors are indicated by 400 error codes. GitHub uses a similar convention for denoting errors.

If a client using the API sends an invalid JSON, a 400 Bad Request response is returned back to the client. If a client using the API misses to send a field as part of the request body, a 422 Unprocessable Entity response is returned to the client.

Rate limiting

The GitHub API also supports rate limiting so that the server is not overburdened with too many requests from some rogue client causing it to fail. In case of requests using **Basic authentication** or **OAuth**, the client is allowed to make up to 5,000 requests per hour. In case of unauthenticated requests, the rate limit is up to 60 requests per hour for a client. GitHub uses the **X-RateLimit-Limit**, **X-RateLimit-Remaining**, and **X-RateLimit-Reset** headers to tell the status of the rate limits.

Thus, we have covered details on the GitHub API on how they choose to implement some of the REST principles we have covered so far in this book. The next section covers the Facebook Open Graph REST API for topics such as versioning, error handling, rate limiting, and so on.

Overview of the Facebook Graph API

The Facebook Graph API is a way to get information from Facebook data. Using the HTTP REST API, clients can do a variety of tasks such as query data, post updates and pictures, get albums and create albums, get the number of likes for a node, get comments, and so on. The following section covers how to get access to the Facebook Graph API.

> On the Web, Facebook uses a variant of the OAuth 2.0 protocol for authentication and authorization. The native Facebook App is used on iOS and Android.

To use the Facebook API, the client needs to procure an access token to work with OAuth 2.0. The following steps shows how to create the App ID and secret key and then get the access token to execute queries for Facebook data:

1. Go to `developers.facebook.com/apps`. You can create a new app. Once the app is created, you will be assigned the App ID and secret as shown in the following screenshot:

2. Once you have the App ID and secret, you can get the access token and execute queries for Facebook data.

Facebook has a special /me endpoint, which corresponds to the user whose access token is being used. To get photos for your user, the request can be of the following form:

GET /graph.facebook.com/me/photos

3. To post a message, the user can invoke a simple API as shown:

    ```
    POST /graph.facebook.com/me/feed?message="foo"
        &access_token="…."
    ```

4. To get details of your ID, name, and photos using the Graph Explorer, the query is as follows:

    ```
    https://developers.facebook.com/tools/explorer?method=GET&path=me%
    3Ffields=id,name
    ```

5. The following screenshot shows a Graph API Explorer query with node dalailama. Clicking on the ID gives more details for the node.

Thus, we saw how to use the Graph API Explorer application to build up a query for a node in the Social Graph. We can query by various fields such as ID and name and try using methods such as GET, POST, or DELETE.

Verbs and resource actions

The following table summarizes the commonly used verbs in the Facebook Graph API:

Verb	Description
GET	This is used to retrieve resources such as feeds, albums, posts, and so on
POST	This is used for creating resources such as feeds, posts, albums, and so on
PUT	This is used for replacing resources
DELETE	This is used for deleting resources

 An important observation is that the Facebook Graph API uses POST instead of PUT to update resources.

Versioning

The Graph API currently uses version 2.1 released on August 7, 2014. The client can specify a version in the request URL. In case a client does not specify a version, the Facebook Open Graph API defaults to the latest version available. Every version is guaranteed to work for 2 years after which if the client makes any calls using an older version, they get redirected to the latest version of the API.

Error handling

The following snippet shows the error response from a failed API request:

```
{
    "error": {
        "message": "Message describing the error",
        "type": "OAuthException",
        "code": 190 ,
        "error_subcode": 460
    }
}
```

As shown in the preceding code, there are JSON Objects called code and error_ subcode in the error message, which can be used to figure out what the problem is and what the recovery action will be. In this case, the value of code is 190, which is an OAuthException value, and the error_subcode value of 460 indicates that the password may have changed and hence the access_token is not valid.

Rate limiting

The Facebook Graph API has different rate-limiting policies based on whether the entity using the API is a user, an application, or an advertisement. When the calls from a user exceed a limit, there is a 30-minute block-out period for the user. For more details, check `https://developers.facebook.com/docs/reference/ads-api/api-rate-limiting/`. The next section covers the details of the Twitter REST API.

Overview of the Twitter API

The **Twitter API** has REST APIs and Streaming APIs, which allow developers to access core data such as timelines, status data, user information, and so on.

Twitter uses three-legged OAuth to make requests.

Important aspects of OAuth with Twitter API

The client application doesn't need to store a login ID and password. The application sends an access token representing the user with each request instead of using user credentials.

The `POST` variables, query parameters, and the URL of the request always remain intact for a request to successfully complete.

The user decides what applications can act on his behalf and can remove authorization at any time.

A unique identifier for each request (the `oauth_nonce` identifier) prevents replaying the same request again in case it gets snooped.

To send requests to Twitter, most developers may find the initial setup a bit confusing. The article at `https://blog.twitter.com/2011/improved-oauth-10a-experience` shows how to create an application, generate the keys, and generate a request using the OAuth tool.

Here is an example of a request generated by the OAuth tool in Twitter, showing a query to get statuses for the `twitterapi` handle:

The Twitter API does not support unauthenticated requests and has very strict rate-limiting policies.

```
curl --get 'https://api.twitter.com/1.1/statuses/user_timeline.
json' --data 'screen_name=twitterapi' --header 'Authorization: OAuth
oauth_consumer_key="w2444553d23cWKnuxrlvnsjWWQ", oauth_nonce="dhg2222324
b268a887cdd900009ge4a7346", oauth_signature="Dqwe2jru1NWgdFIKm9cOvQhghmdP
4c%3D", oauth_signature_method="HMAC-SHA1", oauth_timestamp="1404519549",
oauth_token="456356j901-A880LMupyw4iCnVAm24t33HmnuGOCuNzABhg5QJ3SN8Y",
oauth_version="1.0"'—verbose.
```

This gives an output as shown:

```
GET /1.1/statuses/user_timeline.json?screen_name=twitterapi HTTP/1.1
Host: api.twitter.com
Accept: */*
 HTTP/1.1 200 OK
…
"url":"http:\/\/t.co\/78pYTvWfJd","entities":{"url":{"urls":[{"url
":"http:\/\/t.co\/78pYTvWfJd","expanded_url":"http:\/\/dev.twitter.
com","display_url":"dev.twitter.com","indices":[0,22]}]}},"descriptio
n":{"urls":[]}},"protected":false,"followers_count":2224114,"friends_
count":48,"listed_count":12772,"created_at":"Wed May 23 06:01:13 +0000
2007","favourites_count":26,"utc_offset":-25200,"time_zone":"Pacific Time
(US & Canada)","geo_enabled":true,"verified":true,"statuses_count":351
1,"lang":"en","contributors_enabled":false,"is_translator":false,"is_
translation_enabled":false,"profile_background_color":"C0DEED","profile_
background_image_url":"http:\/\/pbs.twimg.com\/profile_background_
images\/656927849\/miyt9dpjz77sc0w3d4vj….
```

Verbs and resource actions

The following table summarizes the commonly used verbs in the Twitter REST API:

Verb	Description
GET	This is used to retrieve resources such as users, followers, favorites, subscribers, and so on.
POST	This is used to create resources such as users, followers, favorites, subscribers, and so on.
POST with verb update	This is used to replace resources. For example, to update the friendships, the URL will be POST friendships/update.
POST with verb destroy	This is used to delete resources such as deleting direct messages, unfollowing someone, and so on. For example, the URL will be POST direct_messages/destroy.

Versioning

The current version for the Twitter API is 1.1. It only supports JSON and no longer supports XML, RSS, or Atom. With the Twitter API Version 1.1, all clients need to be authenticated using OAuth to make queries. The Twitter API Version 1.0 has been deprecated and there is a 6-month window to move to the new version.

Error handling

The Twitter API returns standard HTTP error codes in the responses to the REST API. It returns `200 OK` in case of success. It returns `304 Not Modified` when there is no data to return, `401 Not Authorized` in case authentication credentials were missing or incorrect, `500 Internal Server Error` when something is broken and needs to be posted to the forum, and so on. Along with detailed error messages, the Twitter API produces machine-readable error codes. For example, an error code `32` in the response implies the server could not authenticate the user. For more details, check `https://dev.twitter.com/docs/error-codes-responses`.

Recommended reading

The following section provides some links, which may be useful to review:

- Facebook Tools: `https://developers.facebook.com/tools/`
- Twurl (OAuth-enabled cURL for Twitter): `https://github.com/twitter/twurl`
- GitHub API documentation: `https://developer.github.com/v3/`
- Twitter API documentation: `https://dev.twitter.com/docs/api/1.1`
- Stripe API documentation: `https://stripe.com/docs/api`

Summary

This appendix is a modest collection of APIs implemented by popular platforms such as GitHub, Facebook, and Twitter and the approaches they have taken to handle the various REST patterns. Though there are a myriad of possibilities for what a user can do with the data from the REST API, the commonality between the frameworks is the usage of REST and JSON. The REST APIs from these platforms are consumed by web and mobile clients. This appendix covered how these platforms handle versioning, verbs, error handling, and authenticating and authorizing the requests based on OAuth 2.0.

This book started off with the basics of REST and how to build your own RESTful services. Since then, we covered various topics as well as tips, and best practices for building scalable and highly performant REST services. We have also referred to various libraries and tools to improve testing and documentation of REST services along with emerging standards for real-time APIs. We also covered case studies with WebSockets, WebHooks, and the future of REST.

We hope this humble attempt from our end helps you understand, learn, design, and develop better REST APIs in the future.

Index

B

basic authentication 118
best practices, logging REST API
  detailed consistent pattern, including
    across service logs 43
  initiator, identifying 44
  logging system, tying with monitoring
    system 44, 45
  log payloads, avoiding 44
  meta-information, identifying of request 44
  sensitive data, obfuscating 44
best practices, OAuth
  encryption, using 57
  lifetime, limiting for access token 56
  providing, support for refresh tokens 56
  SSL, using 57
Bidirectional streams Over Synchronous
    HTTP (BOSH)
  about 109
  advantage 109

C

Cache-Control header
  about 62, 63
  adding, to JAX-RS response 64, 65
  directives 63, 64
caching
  about 58, 62
  benefits 62
  caching headers 62
  RESTEasy 68, 69
caching headers
  about 62
  strong caching headers 62
  weak caching headers 62
ChunkedOutput
  about 32-34
  versus StreamingOutput 34
Client API 18, 19
close function 108
CoffeesResource class 15
CompletionCallback function 70
ConcurrentHashMap class 83
ConnectionCallback function 70
content negotiation
  about 26

performing, based on URL patterns 29, 30
performing, HTTP headers used 27-29
URL 40
Couchbase
  URL 77
cURL 20
cursor-based pagination 90

D

Dapper 45
data masking
  reference link 44
dB 106
DELETE method 14
directives, Cache-Control header
  max-age 63
  no-cache 63
  no-store 63
  private 63
  public 63
doFilter() method 84, 85

E

Emite BOSH library
  URL 112
entity providers 30, 31
entity representation
  about 30, 31
  ChunkedOutput 32-34
  Jersey 34
  StreamingOutput 32
error handling, RESTful services 47, 48
ETag
  about 63-65
  and JAX-RS 67
  Facebook REST API 68
  strongly validating ETag 67, 68
  weakly validating ETag 67, 68
  working with 66
EventSource interface
  about 104
  addEventListener function 104
  onclose function 104
  onerror function 104
  onmessage function 104
  onopen function 104

identity provider (IdP) 50, 51
Instant Payment Notification (IPN) 106
internationalization
  principles 92
InvocationCallback function 70
ISO-3166 country codes
  URL 93
isReadable() method 31
isWritable() method 31

J

Java API for RESTful Services. *See* JAX-RS
JavaScript
  and SSE 104, 105
javax.ws.rs.ApplicationPath annotation 19
javax.ws.rs.client.Client annotation 19
javax.ws.rs.client.WebTarget annotation 19
javax.ws.rs.Consumes annotation 19
javax.ws.rs.ext.ExceptionMapper class 47
javax.ws.rs.Path annotation 19
javax.ws.rs.Produces annotation 19
JAXB-based JSON binding support 34
JAX-RS 15-17
JAX-RS 2.0 15
Jersey
  and OAuth 2.0 56
  and SSE 105
  JSON support 34
  URL, for authorization code grant flow 56
JSONLint
  about 22
  URL 22
JSON Patch
  about 76
  op 76
  path 76
  URL 77
  value 76
JSON Patch RFC 6902
  URL 77
JSON Pointer RFC 6901
  URL 77
JSON support
  JAXB-based JSON binding support 34
  low-level JSON parsing support 35
  low-level JSON processing support 35

POJO-based JSON binding support 34

L

Last-Modified 63, 64
localization parameters 92
logging 58
logging REST API
  about 42
  best practices 43
  creating 42, 43
low-level JSON parsing support 35
low-level JSON processing support 35

M

MessageBodyReader
  about 31
  isReadable() method 31
  readFrom() method 31
MessageBodyWriter
  about 31
  getSize() method 31
  isWritable() method 31
  writeTo() method 31
metadata element 91
method attribute 95
Micro Services, advantages
  clear separation of capabilities 112
  isolation of problems 111
  language independence 112
  scale down 111
  scale up 111
  simplicity 111

O

OAuth
  about 52-54, 118
  advantages 54
  best practices 56
  diagrammatic representation 52
  example 53
  important aspects 122
  versus SAML 57
OAuth 1.0
  differentiating, with OAuth 2.0 54

X

Thank you for buying
RESTful Java Patterns and Best Practices

About Packt Publishing

Packt, pronounced 'packed', published its first book *"Mastering phpMyAdmin for Effective MySQL Management"* in April 2004 and subsequently continued to specialize in publishing highly focused books on specific technologies and solutions.

Our books and publications share the experiences of your fellow IT professionals in adapting and customizing today's systems, applications, and frameworks. Our solution based books give you the knowledge and power to customize the software and technologies you're using to get the job done. Packt books are more specific and less general than the IT books you have seen in the past. Our unique business model allows us to bring you more focused information, giving you more of what you need to know, and less of what you don't.

Packt is a modern, yet unique publishing company, which focuses on producing quality, cutting-edge books for communities of developers, administrators, and newbies alike. For more information, please visit our website: www.packtpub.com.

About Packt Open Source

In 2010, Packt launched two new brands, Packt Open Source and Packt Enterprise, in order to continue its focus on specialization. This book is part of the Packt Open Source brand, home to books published on software built around Open Source licenses, and offering information to anybody from advanced developers to budding web designers. The Open Source brand also runs Packt's Open Source Royalty Scheme, by which Packt gives a royalty to each Open Source project about whose software a book is sold.

Writing for Packt

We welcome all inquiries from people who are interested in authoring. Book proposals should be sent to author@packtpub.com. If your book idea is still at an early stage and you would like to discuss it first before writing a formal book proposal, contact us; one of our commissioning editors will get in touch with you.

We're not just looking for published authors; if you have strong technical skills but no writing experience, our experienced editors can help you develop a writing career, or simply get some additional reward for your expertise.

RESTful Java Web Services Security

ISBN: 978-1-78398-010-9   Paperback: 144 pages

Secure your RESTful applications against common vulnerabilities

1. Learn how to use, configure, and set up tools for applications that use RESTful web services to prevent misuse of resources.

2. Get to know and fix the most common vulnerabilities of RESTful web services APIs.

3. A step-by-step guide portraying the importance of securing a RESTful web service with simple examples applied to real-world scenarios.

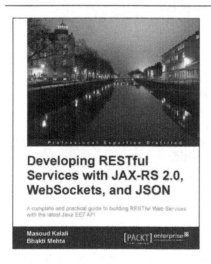

Developing RESTful Services with JAX-RS 2.0, WebSockets, and JSON

ISBN: 978-1-78217-812-5   Paperback: 128 pages

A complete and practical guide to building RESTful Web Services with the latest Java EE7 API

1. Learning about different client/server communication models including but not limited to client polling, server-sent events, and WebSockets.

2. Efficiently use WebSockets, server-sent events, and JSON in Java EE applications.

3. Learn about JAX-RS 2.0 new features and enhancements.

RESTful Java Web Services

ISBN: 978-1-84719-646-0   Paperback: 256 pages

Master core REST concepts and create RESTful web services in Java

1. Build powerful and flexible RESTful web services in Java using the most popular Java RESTful frameworks to date (Restlet, JAX-RS-based frameworks: Jersey and RESTEasy, and Struts 2).

2. Master the concepts to help you design and implement RESTful web services.

3. Plenty of screenshots and clear explanations to facilitate learning.

Developing RESTful Web Services with Jersey 2.0

ISBN: 978-1-78328-829-8   Paperback: 98 pages

Create RESTful web services smoothly using the robust Jersey 2.0 and JAX-RS APIs

1. Understand and implement the Jersey and JAX-RS APIs with ease.

2. Construct top-notch server and client-side web services.

3. Learn about server-sent events, for showing real-time data.

Please check **www.PacktPub.com** for information on our titles

CPSIA information can be obtained at www.ICGtesting.com
Printed in the USA
LVOW03s1532260315

432160LV00020B/970/P

9 781783 287963